Social Media Equals Social Customer

Managing Customer Experience in the Age of Social Media

Donnovan Simon

iUniverse LLC
Bloomington

Social Media Equals Social Customer
Managing Customer Experience in the Age of Social Media

iUniverse books may be ordered through booksellers or by contacting:

iUniverse LLC
1663 Liberty Drive
Bloomington, IN 47403
www.iuniverse.com
1-800-Authors (1-800-288-4677)

ISBN: 978-1-4917-0232-1 (sc)
ISBN: 978-1-4917-0234-5 (hc)
ISBN: 978-1-4917-0233-8 (ebk)

Library of Congress Control Number: 2013914681

Printed in the United States of America

iUniverse rev. date: 08/16/2013

Social Media Equals Social Customer

CONTENTS

Preface...vii
Introduction..ix

Chapter 1   The Social Customer.............................1
Chapter 2   What Customers See and Hear................7
Chapter 3   Social Media, Social Customer.............20
Chapter 4   How Social Customers Speak...............35
Chapter 5   Generation Gaps.................................45
Chapter 6   Social Customers Equals Higher Expectations....55
Chapter 7   Getting the Social Customer to Stay.................66
Chapter 8   Customer Service 2.0..........................76
Chapter 9   Customer Experience Management..................89
Chapter 10   What Next?.......................................100

Acknowledgements..115

Appendices
        Appendix 1   My Survey Results.............................119
        Appendix 2   Description of Top 10 Social
                     Networking Sites................................123

Works Cited...129
Notes...131

PREFACE

This book is about things that are already happening in some organizations. It's also about how customers are changing. Companies thrive because of customers. Many companies benefit from social technologies, and some have made billions from it. But some companies have not, and do not immediately plan to make appropriate adjustments to deal with the demands the current and next generation of customers make. I am confident that my kids' generation will make life very exciting yet challenging for business leaders. To that extent, I want to provoke thought and action around some key areas of business. I hope this will drive deeper strategic thinking that will be translated into concrete programs and plans. If I can achieve that with this book, I would feel that I have made a meaningful contribution to the growth of an organization and the career of a well-intended professional who did not have the time and foresight to explore these issues.

My interest in the discipline of supporting customers continues to grow. After writing *The Way You Make Me Feel: 20 Lessons in Customer Service* (2011), I spent more time looking at the way companies approached crucial strategies on how to support customers in ways that were fiscally responsible, yet satisfying to those receiving the service offerings. From the research done for this book, it was apparent to me that many companies had not forged ahead with the appropriate investments to meet customers in the spaces where they preferred, and therefore they lost customers to companies who were more aware. It was also obvious to me that the landscape had changed so dramatically that many companies were at different stages of accepting and responding to the changes. Some were in denial and were struggling to accept the realities that propelled the new world. I have watched my six-year-old daughter, Danielle, surf the Internet, navigate an iPad, and manipulate a smartphone with ease and innate expertise. This experience made me believe that the taboo, fear, and intimidation that limited the transformation of those of my generation do not exist for the consumers of today and tomorrow. Other parents have corroborated my observation and are anxious to see how our kids, the customers of today and tomorrow, will adapt to the next great gadget. This is the world we do business in.

This book is about how to support the next generation of consumers whose demands and expectations are significantly different. It will take very different skills, structures, and strategies to be successful. It will be exhilarating to watch as the forces of supply and demand, customer and supplier, employer and employee, duel to the happy end. In the process there will surely be winners and losers. What is more sure, even if it is only a conservative bet, is that the consumer will win more times than not and in many cases the challenge will be lopsided. With that result comes an equally exciting challenge for business owners and managers who will need to navigate these waters to deliver shareholder value and profits. The following chapters are geared to providing context and helping to make it easier for those with such responsibilities.

INTRODUCTION

Being inclined towards technology and having a desire to be digitally social are characteristics of today's generation that those who are "old school" don't always understand. Often the youth opt more, to apply shortened, quicker versions of the same methodology used by their predecessors to achieve the same outcomes. Isn't that true? They communicate through symbols and acronyms that baffle their parents. What they have done is part of a revolution that has pushed the boundaries of customer demand to new levels. These customers have also created a dramatic pull factor within many industries. Many companies are part of this revolution that are on the edge and appeal to this ever-broadening population of savvy, impatient consumers. Some companies lag behind the wave and are slow to adopt and adapt to the new flavours within consumerism. They are missing out on possibilities.

The rapid growth of social media has forced everyone to stop and take note. The constant reference to the many social technologies used by so many leaves one to marvel at the impact and necessity of these tools, which amplify customer voices. Previously, the voice of the customer was received through traditional means such as surveys. These were costly, time-consuming exercises that, although well-intentioned, captured a perspective at a point in time and were always accompanied by the caveat of the error tolerance of the results. Today, the dynamic world of Web 2.0 adds an exciting new dimension to how customers are perceived and how their voice is captured. [1] The advent of these technologies has ensured a constant flow of customer feedback and input. Consumer silence has been eliminated. Globally, at any time, millions of customers share their views, both solicited and unsolicited, through social media. As the wheels of industry turn, so does the voice of the customer.

To support business leaders and customer support practitioners who are listening to these voices, this book will

- Provide data and context around social networking trends
- Show the correlation between the trends and new customer personas
- Suggest strategic elements for businesses to consider to effectively tackle the trends
- Provide ideas on how to deliver the best experience for customers using social media

Social media has created a new sense of power for the consumer who, at any time, can influence activities, thoughts, and strategies in diverse parts of the world. The launch, success, and occasional failure of a product can be accelerated or delayed through the impact of social media. The founders of Facebook, Twitter, YouTube, and other social media platforms may not have intended to influence the world the way they have. Rather, the platforms may have been a way to facilitate communication while making money. However, they are now mega-players in an industry that thrives on the power of virtual objects. The social media platforms are change agents and their ideas are consumed by millions daily. Greater yet, consumers keep coming back for more.

The frenzy in social media does mean many organizations need to change strategy, especially those who appeal to a certain demographic and whose products and services naturally complement technology. For example, a newspaper or publishers must accept that the growth of the Internet creates an expectation that their products will be available online 24/7 with global reach. The same applies to airlines, brand-name department stores, and many other industries. It is now normal for customers to have that expectation, and anything less is frowned upon. Additionally, once established in this technology domain, customers expect that the traditional way of listening will change. Online, social media-ready tools become more crucial compared to methods that do not result in instant feedback like direct mail.

With all the changes, customer service professionals need to adjust and find ways to stay with and ahead of the pace. The strategies applied will either contribute to an organization being considered part of the magic quadrant and therefore maintaining competitive advantage or be in the circle with the laggards and consistently lose ground. While the task is by no means easy or inexpensive, strategy makers, managers, and influencers will be able to integrate some fundamental components presented here into strategies already developed or being developed. Ideally, this will contribute to providing consistent quality experiences that customers expect.

Some things will remain constant in any customer satisfaction equation, no matter the different technologies that abound. One factor will be the customer voice. Customers will continue to share their opinions with businesses in various ways, some overt and well-articulated, others buried in subtle actions and innuendos. Social media has added a new layer to this situation. What the discerning organization and associated management teams will be forced to do is adjust strategies to accommodate the impact of the new customer types created by social media. This will be more important as customer sensitivity about their value to businesses continues to increase. Businesses may need to spend more managing heightened customer expectations, and customer retention. Staff who interact directly with these customers must be capable of making the types of decisions required to meet both customer and business expectations. Having these skills available will reduce the cost to provide service and also ensure that customers develop confidence in the organization's culture and brand.

While some organizations adapting to social media may require revolution and transformation, others are already in line with if not ahead of some of what the typical customer seeks. As the digital age drives the digital generation to live further on the edge of innovation, customers will expect that the tools available to meet their purchasing needs will be optimized to meet their support needs. If purchasing via a mobile device is available, then the expectation is that after-sales support would be accessible through that platform. It would be deemed not only damaging to an organization's competitive placement to ignore the digital generation, but also foolish to miss the power and financial potential of the trend of digital convergence that occurs with mobile devices. The fact that a mobile phone has evolved to being a "smart" phone is an opportunity that organizations must acknowledge and cater to in order to effectively hear, interact, and satisfy customer expectations. The evolution is by no means over and the power that it may bring to the customer may, for some, seem like an unfair advantage. In the minds of many, it is the way it is, and likely to be with us for a long time. This book is geared to people who have the difficult task of being part of the customer experience equation, no matter the role. The changes happening every day must be reviewed to ensure that any gains made are not only maintained but also built upon to drive organizational success.

CHAPTER 1
The Social Customer

We are in an era where systems, processes, and products are being developed to meet the tastes of individuals whose distinctive feature is the fact that they practice social networking. A lot is being invested to understand these new individuals and the implications for business strategies, processes, and practices. The new persona, often described as the "social customer," has become the focus of attention for analysts, marketers, and executives in an attempt to understand this person and guide organizations in the best way to successfully deal with this type of customer.

Who is a social customer?

Do you pay for your coffee using your smartphone? Have you ever felt deprived when you cannot tweet at will? Do you check products online before going to the mall? How much of your shopping is done online? Depending on your responses, you may be a social customer. Social customers actively use social networking technologies and transfer many of the attributes related to social networking to the way they consume goods and services. The social customer is normally:

- Completing business transactions online
- Applying social media language to consumption processes
- Sharing or collecting information related to consumption activities within social networks
- Applying ratings to products and services via social media
- Establishing interactions, where possible, with organizations and other customers via social media

While there are more attributes that are unique to different individuals, in this chapter we will discuss some consistent practices that reflect the persona. Some important distinctions need to be made from the outset to ensure that we appreciate the differences contained in this persona.

1. A social customer is not bound by an age group. While we will discuss the differences between generations, it is critical to accept that being a Millennial does not make one an automatic social customer. In the same breath, many Baby Boomers are strong social customers. 2. The phenomenon is global. Social customers are as prevalent in China as they are in the United States, despite the differences in culture and socio-economic practices. Social customers transcend many of the barriers (age, income, education, geography, etc.) that may have previously impacted personas. Many persons may not consider themselves social customers, or vice versa, but they display all the characteristics of one. This may be due to personal views and the disinclination of some individuals to being lumped in with

stereotypes or trends. Nevertheless, the reality is they operate actively in social spheres and behave consistently with other people who choose to operate in a virtual world.

3. The social customer is still evolving. Likely new dimensions of the persona will become important with time as technology and its application continue to influence the way people live and conduct business.

Social customers have consistent attributes, but also differences in how individuals choose to act. This is no different than any other customer segment. Essentially, the category of social customer has many different types. Michael Brito identifies six types in his work *The Rise of the Social Customer and their Impact on Business,* as follows: [2]

- The Venting Customer
- The Passive Customer
- The "Used to Be" Customer
- The Collaborative Customer
- The Customer Advocate
- The Future Customer

These types can be personified in a many different ways. I reference them to show that as we examine the concept of the social customer, many different behaviours occur that represent segments of the social customer constituency. These different behaviours validate the difficult challenge business leaders are forced to be aware of and respond to. Additionally, the basic personalities of customers remain despite social media. The strategies being devised to address the era of the social customer must reflect an appreciation of the fact that some elements of supporting and delighting customers are standard, no matter the social era. It leaves an important question open for discussion: Are expectations different in the era of the social customer?

Simple and complex responses can be given to this question. The simple response would be that customer expectations remain the same. All customers want to receive value, be treated respectfully, and have issues resolved quickly. In any era, those expectations would standard. However, higher minimum expectations are consistently being set in the era of the social customer. These expectations are products of the powerful voice that social media provides customers and the behaviours associated with social media use. Rachel Tran states that customers have three main expectations of companies using social media, as follows:[3]

- **Be fast**. A social customer service team's performance can be measured by its response times and the number of queries answered.
- **Be useful**. First contact resolution from customer service is the key to customer satisfaction. The right tools and processes help companies to get queries to the right team member as quickly as possible so that helpful answers can be delivered through social media.
- **Be friendly**. Tone of voice is the most important and the most difficult challenge to master for social customer service teams. It's important to deliver genuine, professional help while maintaining the way customers reach out through social platforms.

When we examine the items above, we can see that nothing fundamental has changed in what customers, social or otherwise, are looking for from organizations that provide goods and services. The fact that they may choose to transact via a mobile device, PC, or in person has not changed the basic expectations that rational customers have always had. It is also reasonable to deduce that it should not change the basic offerings that companies should include as part of the products they bring to market. However, customers are demanding more. In upcoming chapters, we will discuss how the social nature of customers drives the desire for increased speed and access, which fuels an increase in expectations. This is where the complexity in the response comes in because while base expectations are unchanged, how customer satisfaction is measured has changed in some areas. The expectation for speed has increased. The expectation for new social support channels, like Twitter, has increased. In a survey reported by *SocialBusinessNews.com*, 81 percent of Twitter users expect a same-day response to questions and complaints asked through that platform.[4]

The concept of the social customer has global application. Customers in all regions are actively participating in social media and are displaying characteristics common to those attuned to being online. For example, in China the use of instant messaging is a significant part of online activity. Top Chinese Internet provider Tencent reports over 370 million monthly users for their QQ messaging service. According to China Internet Watch's report *China Social Media Whitepaper* (October 2012), there were over 300 million active social media users in China with over 50 percent of them browsing social media via smartphones.[5] The same trends are being seen in India, Brazil, Australia, the United Kingdom, and the United States.

The proliferation of social customers globally does not mean they all behave the same way. It is important to understand and accept that cultural norms strongly influence customer behaviour. In a highly litigious and outspoken society like the United States, it is normal for social customers to use social media as part of the process of challenging organizations, including government, or exposing their dissatisfaction with an organization's product or service. On the contrary, although equally or more active in social media, the same does not occur in Chinese culture. Are they all social customers? Yes, but their practices are distinctly different. Why is this important to discuss in the context of this book? Because organizations that operate globally may miss the need to acknowledge the cultural nuances that apply to digital natives and therefore miss opportunities to structure their support systems to deliver the desired experience in each culture.

While many questions still are not completely answered relating to social customers, the reality is that social customers exist in various types and are influencing businesses and business practices globally. Through the data, ideas, and questions in the other chapters, I hope that those people involved in the development and implementation of customer support strategies will add some of these elements to their success equations to equip their teams to be more successful. Success will be determined by the way these customers respond, and it is likely to be consistent with their social media behaviour.

CHAPTER 2
What Customers See and Hear

I came home from work one day to meet my very excited six-year-old daughter Danielle at the door with an urgent need for my credit card. She wanted to purchase the most amazing exercise machine she had seen on the Internet. I was fascinated that she was so sure it was the best thing for me, but also keen to understand who would have marketed such a machine on a site my six-year-old would be on. Sure enough, the machine was there and I got the message. Strategies are being employed in many different ways to trigger the senses of customers and influencers; even if it means reaching the target in an indirect way.

Today's consumer has a luxury of riches in terms of the many sources available to see or hear about a product or service. Information, advice, pricing, competitive comparison, or other details are readily available. Over time, various technologies have been developed to distribute messages to large audiences in short periods of time. Communicating through newspaper, radio, television, outdoor billboards, and other mass media methods can lead to consumers being bombarded yet informed. The arrival of the Internet began an era of transformation in the customers' favour. What started as a way to provide and prove connectivity exploded into a communications phenomenon the world had not previously imagined. Then came mobile telephones. The convergence of devices followed: the pager, address book, and website were available in one gadget. The optimization of devices and networks came next. Today, and who knows for tomorrow, people are inclined to socialize through converged devices and networks.

New technology has made it easier for people to communicate, increasing the ability to reach more people quickly. Consequently, companies have invested significantly to manage the impact of these technologies on consumers. With television, radio, newspapers, and other basic advertising media all converging, customers now have the option to hear and see everything they previously received from multiple sources, on a single device. In effect, a single source of information and communication has been created. The terms radio, television, and newspaper have become nominally inaccurate as they describe sources rather than hardware or communications technologies, which they previously were. If you can tune into the same program on your mobile phone or other devices as you can on your television set, what does that say about television hardware? I can get radio stations on the Internet. Does that make my computer a radio? The same applies to television, which can now be accessed through a mobile phone. Is a mobile phone a television? The social era has transformed mass media methods into simply video, data, and text. TV, radio, and newspaper represent the language of the past.

While we unravel that confusion, there is no doubt that consumers are raising their championship belt and proclaiming victory, or at least a sense of triumph because of the power they've acquired. What may have appeared a distant achievement has become mainstream and the power of consumers is reflected in the fact that trillions of dollars are spent globally to reach them. Through various methods, consumers are "seeing and hearing" what different sellers want them to see and hear. The intended reward for the sellers is obvious—more revenue. The gain for consumers is also fairly straightforward—better prices, more, and in some cases, better products. While this all unfolds, connecting with, hearing, and effectively supporting the customer is also changing dramatically. What was a basic element of business has increased complexity significantly. Customer support options have to be constantly monitored, measured, and managed. In many organizations, resources are being assigned new roles to ensure that consumers are being catered to in the way they like and that they are getting the most from the products they invested in. Businesses, their processes, and outlook are also being transformed. Changing customers, with their actions and preferences, are significant drivers to these changes. Social technologies are a big part of the changes. One example of this could be the success of online search engines. People always want to find something on the Internet. In response, the idea of a search tool to help Internet users identify providers of goods, services, or information has been transformed into an extremely successful industry. The search technologies and the Internet are now critical to how customers are supported.

There is no contest when comparing the success of Google to that of the largest media companies. In 2011, Google reported revenues of USD$36.5 billion, which represented a 23 percent growth from the USD$26.3 billion reported in 2010.[6] Many other successful companies are in the business of helping customers find what they need in the "virtual" world. Facebook, LinkedIn, and YouTube are all representative of the shift and success in the way businesses are forced to consider how customers see and hear them. LinkedIn, which went public in 2011, has seen revenue grow from $120 million in 2009 to $522 million in 2011. Traditional media organizations (newspapers, radio, and television) are not showing the same trends. The growth of what I call "new media" is positive for a global economy that has had to deal with a range of different shocks and stutter-steps. The fact that social media businesses have become cornerstones of the way people work, interact, and connect is indicative of the value created and offered by these "new media" companies. They have become a core part of people's lives globally. This global impact is reported in numerous surveys relating to the changes caused by these social media sites and their convergence with other technological occurrences.

The significance of the role of these companies and technologies in how news, data, and information are distilled globally can be examined through various lenses. YouTube, which was acquired by Google in 2006, has two billion views daily, with 60 hours of video uploaded every minute. Facebook reaches 73 percent of Internet users in the United States daily. The data continues to astound in terms of the scope and reach of these tools—yes—tools. Users are able to cover almost all areas of the globe with news and information in milliseconds through these tools. To add another perspective, a standard acceptance and expectation is that people should connect using these tools. Recently, American pop star Justin Timberlake, after a few years of not releasing a new album, relied on Twitter to alert the world of the impending release of his new single. No press conference. No press release. No website update or fancy declaration through traditional media. A tweet did it. His post, powered by the social jet streams, was able to break records and had over 400,000 downloads within a day of release. It was not the traditional marketing genius spinning messages and building appealing images. It capitalized on a social media ocean with global reach, powerful waves, and eager recipients.

These "new media" tools have overlapped to ensure that the world is interrelated and interconnected seamlessly. Messages through these channels automatically have a viral feature that can be exploited by both companies and individuals. Social tools are now a significant part of the customer experience cycle. The shift in the structure of how consumers are communicated with has a direct impact on how they are eventually supported. Their engagement begins through the different media that they connect with in the dynamic world of social technologies and contributes to the formation of experiences. The other stages in the customer experience cycle must therefore be in sync to capitalize on the gains made in the engagement phase. The impact of both message and media continue way past that phase. Since the customer experience contributes to business success, we should examine the impact of messages being shared across different media. The entire customer experience should be examined, not just the customer service element. Customers' experiences are being shaped by what they are seeing and hearing all the time. It happens even more as they shift to using social media as a primary source for news, information, and entertainment.

As shifts occur in how customers see and hear, opportunities abound in how to drive the structure, timing, and reach of key messages. Organizations must understand how dissemination and consumption occur in a world built on and driven by technology that encourages social connections. While the traditional functions of media and marketing remain relevant, what people value and believe, from what they see and hear, are often based on the sources from which the information is delivered. Customers are increasingly hearing from their communities. They see and hear from companies but often go back to their networks for validation and details. The functions responsible for and involved in the customer experience process must adapt to this new environment and understand how customers are hearing and seeing things that are important to them and the corporate enterprise. Many companies are already making changes by adjusting channels used to reach customers. The graph below provides interesting data and perspective on how traditional and contemporary investment in advertising (in the United States) reflects the changes being discussed.[7]

Graph 1: U.S. print vs. online ad spending 2011-2016

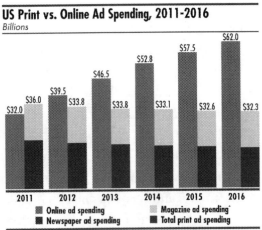

Source: eMarketer Jan 2012

There is no question that the focus on "being where people are" is understood. Connecting via social platforms is now fundamental. The fact that companies like Google and Facebook are able to generate billions of dollars in advertising revenue is indicative of the focus on meeting and attracting customers in the places that they frequent.

To extend the perspective on this issue, investment in advertising through traditional print media, such as newspapers and magazines, is projected to remain flat for the immediate future; this is something to note. There remains an audience for those products, despite the exponential growth and business case around online methods. Similarly, there remains a place for television advertising as not everyone has migrated to all social media. And not everyone is a social customer. As Graph 2 shows, buoyancy is projected in that industry. What is important to acknowledge as we examine this is that the convergence of the various technologies now blurs the lines around how customers see and hear things.

Graph 2: U.S. TV vs. online ad spending
2011-2016 in $ billions (USD)

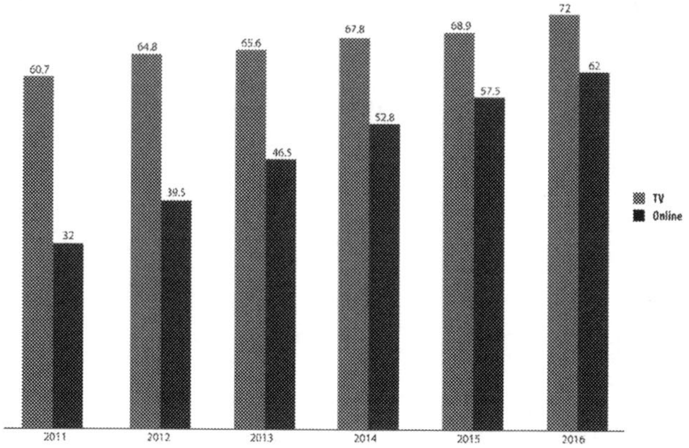

Note:eMarketer benchmarks its US online ad spending projections agains the IAB/PwC data, for which the last full year measured was 2010.

Source: eMarketer Jan 2012

A television ad is now viewed on personal computers, tablets, and smartphones. The distinction between online and television is likely to disappear in the near future. Social media, mobile devices, the borderless world plus blurred lines between media are customer experiences impacting issues that companies will need to grapple with. Companies operating in multiple markets and countries are forced to continuously deal with this challenge. A good example is the recent situation with the new Boeing 787 Dreamliner aircraft. An issue with an aircraft operated in Japan (Nippon Airways) was instantly shared with companies and customers in other markets served by the aircraft. The Boeing 787 is currently flown by United Airlines in the United States and Quantas in Australia. Boeing's customers, United Airlines and Quantas, and their customers, received information and news through multiple convergent sources. People globally could readily see, hear, and share about the issue.

How are customers and prospects responding?

With all the sources available to customers, there must be questions regarding impact and acceptance. With every new community post, blog, or tweet is it likely that the message was not heard? Or if it was heard, did it produce the intended outcome? What are people saying? In a recent survey that I conducted with members of my LinkedIn network, 80 percent stated that they did not respond to advertising on social networks.[8] The majority (55 percent) of the respondents used social media very often (read as daily). Many users of social networking sites feel the same way. It could be concluded that while companies continue to invest in advertising using these platforms, the effect of the advertising investment may not be at optimized levels. Still, it is important to distinguish between advertising and other messages that are communicated through social media. Many different messages get communicated and consumed this way. Customers are able to see and hear more than just glittering advertisements. Corporate news, customer feedback, and market opinions are all easily posted and shared. Maybe most importantly, people share their experiences with their networks. Some of what is shared is about good and bad experiences with companies. Thirty percent of the respondents to my survey used social media to share ideas, news, and information.

As more messages get to customers through social platforms, it is important for organizations to examine and act on customer responses. Why? There may be deviations between intended and actual customer responses, which may require a company response to clarify the initial message. The possibility exists that social noise may distort the transmission of messages, which fuels behaviours and expectations in customers that are not fully supported by the offerings from companies.

Globally, expectations are the same

Many other messages may be extracted from the sights and sounds influencing social customers. Commonly, these messages have some element of universal validity. I have no doubt that an Internet user in Nigeria or some remote part of India has similar expectations of Facebook or Pinterest as a user of similar demographics in the heart of New York. Why shouldn't they? Both are part of a virtual community that sheds the traits and limitations that location would previously drive. After all, they likely use the same hardware, download the same apps and have the same interests. If they invested in being heavily connected, as many do, they would also see the activities of others in their communities since the social platforms provide that opportunity for all users. Everyone gets and expects similar options. The individual in Nigeria may be focused on consumption, as is the user in New York. It does not matter. Most social media users are mainly consumers anyway.

Data shows that the majority of active Internet users are consumers of content versus creators.[9] The expectation of the consumers is that their needs are understood. They also maintain the expectation that more content will be available to them. This expectation is fueled by the fact that there is an app, or web-based tool, for everything imaginable. Interestingly, these apps are not being created by hardware or network providers. Everywhere, and that is to be taken literally, there is an app creator who sees a community that will find value in his or her offering. How else would the consumer derive optimum value from their devices if there was not a game, calorie tracker, tax calculator, QR code reader, simulator, and life planner available to support the power of the device? Consequently, app stores and software developer kits (SDK) are available to support the demand from consumers. The outcome is the proliferation of apps to satisfy varying tastes. The social customer wins, as do different players in the value chain. This development reflects the fact that there is a keen focus on facilitating customers via the media through which they see and hear things.

With the proliferation of devices and social networks come opportunities. This cannot be denied. These opportunities are characterized by many things: ease of entry and exit, rapid growth or demise, huge profits or losses, grand innovation or shameless plagiarism. Customers see the fierce competition in the market and in many cases are aware that they are the drivers. The features that have become common in many products are by no means surprising. For example, nearly all consumer electronics in recent years have included touch and sensory elements. Video and data transmission are standard. Wireless connectivity is standard. As products continue to do more, consumers continue to expect more. With all the advertising and other sources of messages that customers are faced with, it is understandable that they are raising their expectations and using the methods available to them to make companies aware of how they feel. How companies respond is also easily seen and heard, which in some cases provides the social customer with more leverage to rationalize expectations. The social networking platforms provide a framework that facilitates a conversation between customer and company, allowing both to be seen and heard.

The description of what is happening via social media may suggest that there is utter chaos or confusion and that customers and businesses are in the midst of a tornado with no sense of control or influence. I actually believe the opposite because there is an understanding of what is happening. The speed of change is not a fear factor but is expected. Many customers thrive on the way social media has changed how they see and hear.

Those trying to capitalize on the social wave and the era of the customer are usually conscious of the power of getting there first. In many cases, it is a one-shot opportunity to capture the interest of customers. The power of the connections and the viral effect become components of the equation and companies are finding ways to capitalize on these social networks. Increasingly, customers are being encouraged to share, although not in the traditional "word of mouth" sense since that would be too slow in the virtual world. A tweet, Facebook post, blog, or statement in any social community is the new power of "a few words." Sharing, or the request to, is something customers are being asked to do more often. They are also being asked to express their digital emotions. The social customer hears so much from different networks that it has become standard behaviour and expectation. In the last 18 months, nearly every Internet property I have been on has a "like" or "share" option. Why? More customers express their emotions within their social networks and do the same on other sites. These emotional indicators are seen as opportunities to capitalize and create lots of data that allow companies to do extensive analytics. They open a new trend of understanding the customer more, which provides a competitive advantage.

> *"The prosperity of a firm is directly linked to the prosperity of its network. As the platform or standard it operates on flourishes, so does the firm."*
>
> Kelly, Kevin, *New Rules for the New Economy*, Viking Penguin, New York, 1998

Understandably, in a fiercely competitive environment companies are keen to find and use every chance for competitive advantage. In a later chapter, customer loyalty and its impact on success in a borderless world will be examined.

As companies develop strategies for success in the era of the social customer, there must be focus and investment to understand what they are seeing and hearing. This includes greater focus on not only acquiring feedback, ideas, and feelings, but the appropriate responses and processes to support customers. While customers may be happy to engage companies through the social platforms where they see and hear things, they expect companies to respond and acknowledge that the social platforms are legitimate sources of value to companies and customers. Customers want to be heard via these channels.

The value of understanding what customers are seeing and hearing increases as the use of social media grows. In many cases, the success of organizations is significantly impacted by the power of the prevailing technologies in the social media space. Additionally, business leaders, managers, and support professionals are being pulled into the social media networks and are expected to be active participants. Some have proactively taken the plunge. For those who had always advocated the need for customer-centricity, the changes and demands being driven by social networks are welcome. Customers will continue to share via these platforms. They will also hear more, and companies that acknowledge this and respond positively will be on the leading edge of the curve and derive positive benefits. In chapter 5, I will discuss the impact of the different generations on this prognosis and examine how effective strategies can be developed to address the expectations and generational idiosyncrasies that have evolved with the times.

CHAPTER 3
Social Media, Social Customer

I am sure those who devised and designed the Internet or mobile phones did not have social media as part of their vision. The evolution and convergence that has occurred to create the all-pervasive concept of social media is nothing short of magical. Equally amazing is the global impact and importance that it has attained. A significant portion of the world's population has touched and been impacted by social media. Through appeals for aid, activism for environmental issues, promotion of social causes, or merely to expose novel concepts, all nations have at some point been featured in social media. It has been a key part of the transformation in the way the world works, transacts, and connects. The market value of the key players in the sector reflects the view of the money markets on the value and potential of the concepts and technologies. There is no guarantee that it will always be that way. However, it could be argued that the impact that search engine innovator Google has had on business and personal use of the Internet could be eclipsed by the proponents of social media tools and practices. Even if they don't, it is clear that social media has had a dramatic impact on the world.

With that landscape in mind, managers of enterprises, small businesses, and even sole proprietors are challenged to lock into the power and value of social media. For different reasons, businesses need to understand the concept, how it proliferates, how it generates value, and how it creates and fuels change. It would be foolhardy to accept that only positive outcomes have been achieved through social media, therefore managers have to study all the angles that come with the phenomenon to ensure that appropriate actions are taken to meet the requirements of driving their business forward. Failure to ensure that these issues are acknowledged could result in an imbalanced focus and investments that are misaligned with requirements to succeed. The challenge for business leaders is compounded by the speed at which the phenomenon moves. It evolves so quickly that delay could put an organization at a significant disadvantage relative to its competitors. Similarly, the optimization could be so dramatic that an organization could struggle to contain the success derived. This is by no means an effort to exaggerate the impact of social media, as it may, for the average customer and company, be average in its overall impact. However, it cannot be denied that customers are making it a factor in the way they live and operate.

The table below provides an estimate of the number of registered users for the top 10 social networking platforms globally. Further details are contained in Appendix 2. These 10 sites alone attract approximately 3.5 billion, and growing, users globally. This indicates the appeal and value of these sites. It is important to recognize that these sites have grown dramatically in the last 10 years. Facebook, which started in 2004, has almost doubled its user base annually. The success of Facebook was such that the financial markets placed record value on the company. Its IPO was one of the most talked about in recent times.[10] Whether it can maintain its growth rate and profitability and deliver financial value to investors is left to be seen. What is clear is that consumers globally have established Facebook and many other sites offering the opportunity to share, interact, and virtualize the socialization process as a core part of their existence.

Table 1—Top social networking sites by registered users[11]

Name	Registered users[12] in millions
1. Facebook	1,000
2. Qzone	531
3. Twitter	500
4. Google+	500
5. Habbo	273
6. LinkedIn	200
7. Renren	160
8. Badoo	133
9. Bebo	117
10. Vkontakte	110

All these companies, i.e., social networking sites, to varying degrees have become consumer staples, creating numerous other opportunities for advertisers and anyone wanting to reach a mass audience. The appeal of these platforms dissects multiple demographics and geographic zones. Today, marketing and communications automatically include strategies to connect through these media.

Although the focus of this book is not on the presence and proliferation of social media, it is important to establish context. My focus is on who, where, and how social media is being used and the intersection of the phenomenon with other technologies and business disciplines. Ultimately, I want to understand what is happening, how it affects customers' experiences, and how to build strategies to make these experiences outstanding and profitable. We know social media is a core part of the life of millions of individuals who are customers, which suggests that something can be learned from the overlap of roles. This understanding could benefit business leaders as they try to grow their businesses. Additionally, my goal is to analyze opportunities that are steadily being created by social media to determine the most successful ways to optimize their impact on customer experience. I hope that the analysis will provide further perspectives and data on the impact social media continues to have on the relationship between customers and businesses. This would help organizations understand nuances in the application of social media.

In China, for example, where Facebook is banned, there is a different approach to the use of social media versus the United States where there is greater freedom of use. Despite this polarity or perceived polarity, hundreds of millions of Chinese use social media sites. The proliferation of mobile technology in China makes the demand for and use of social media a natural extension. As the economy fuels the adoption of more mobile technologies, there will be more demand and desire by consumers to optimize their devices. This will be reflected in increased use of social networking applications. The reality of having more mobile devices and increased use of these technologies will fuel social pressure for greater acceptance and use of social media. Many other countries experience similar trends that reflect that the concept is universal, even if the purposes for which these platforms are used vary by countries and regions. The phenomenon has been an epidemic and connects people who want to connect.

A parallel to the social networking revolution is the transformation of existing customers into social customers. As discussed in chapter 1, social customers are active participants in social media who demonstrate social media practices and tendencies when they operate as a customer. This persona

> **Who is the Social Customer?**
>
> "Anyone who talks about products or services, online or off."
>
> Michael Brito, *The Rise of the Social Customer and Their Impact on Business,* 2012

has become increasingly evident globally. New products and services continue to appear in response to the rate of growth and consequent opportunities in social media. For some countries and markets, the social media pace of activity continues to be frenetic.

A major part of the phenomenon is the communities that are being formed. As with apps, there is a social community for everything imaginable. Some argue that the core driver is the natural tendency for humans to be social. A simple look at the development of societies shows people innately come together in a single location, with communities forming organically. They then evolve into fully functioning economies. With time, the osmosis that occurs through these processes fuels innovation and enterprise leading to growth, wealth, and human comfort.

People benefit from these communities and are inclined to contribute to their development and maintenance. They pay taxes, volunteer, and donate their resources to support their communities. Economic growth brings growth in technology with social media one of many areas of technological growth. The growth in technology that fuelled social media continues to drive transformation. Consequently, this adds the social media revolution into the mix of business strategy, applicable from the perspective of opportunities created and changes required to extract the benefits that come with the opportunities.

As the Internet transformed to become more interactive and social, creating Web 2.0, it pulled organizations that previously enjoyed its static nature in a new direction. Web 2.0 is merely the optimization of the Internet and the connection of technologies to "virtualize" what has occurred naturally for centuries. While the pace with which the virtual globe is being created is supersonic relative to the cycles for creating the physical world, it should be no surprise. As with the creation of physical communities, virtual, social communities create new forms of consumption that fuel innovative products offering improvement in lifestyles. Many other factors are part of the equation around the growth of communities. My intention is not to perform an analysis of that process but to establish the parallel to what social media has done. Hopefully, accepting the dynamics of the process, whether physical or virtual, creates a number of outcomes, including new types of products and new types of customers. With new products and types of customers have come new service standards and approaches to satisfy the needs of these customers.

Smartphones, tablets, and more connections

Social media has not only fostered innovation, it has spurred other growth areas. The growth of the use of mobile devices, including smartphones, is one such area. As Table 2 shows, there is significant penetration of mobile devices in all regions.

Table 2—Top 10 mobile markets by number of subscriptions

	Country	Mobile subscriptions (in millions)	Population (in millions)	3G/4G subscriptions (in millions)
1	China	1,091.9	1,344.1	212.0
2	India	906.6	1241.0	70.6
3	United States	321.7	311.6	256.0
4	Indonesia	260.0	242.3	47.6
5	Brazil	259.3	196.7	65.5
6	Russia	227.1	141.9	27.0
7	Japan	128.4	127.8	104.4
8	Pakistan	120.5	176.7	N/A
9	Germany	114.2	81.7	53.2
10	Nigeria	143.0	162.5	10.5
Source: IDC report (Aug 2012)			via mobiThinking.com	

Note: Information on 3G stats are forecasted estimates for December 2012

In some cases, there are more mobile phones in a country than the population. This may appear unusual but is quite normal depending on the market. In Jamaica, where I grew up, I was surprised at the number of people who owned phones with different carriers. It was a way to manage costs based on the interconnect rate structure. People could connect with family and friends on one carrier without the extra cost of interconnection.

The immediate future for mobile phones remains positive. The future is even brighter because the mobility enables access to social platforms, so people keen to social network are no longer tied to a computer. The power is now in the consumer's hand. The users of these devices, in many cases, represent the persona of the customer being courted by businesses globally. The demand for devices is also driven by the fact that these users crave the opportunity to stay connected, but not through the traditional voice-based connection. People want to connect with their virtual communities to share and consume information on current situations as it is important to stay current. A smartphone offers that opportunity and therefore meets the varied needs of these users. Not to mention that it serves as an alarm clock, address book, calculator, gaming machine, and more. Today, more than one billion smartphones are in operation with a forecast for the number doubling by 2015.[13] The first smartphone was introduced by Nokia in 1996 and took a while to catch on. The market for these devices is currently worth over US$200 billion with the prediction that by 2016, two-thirds of all mobile phones will be smartphones.

It is important to accept that this is a global concept as represented by the data in Table 3. What the data also alludes to is the likely similarity of customer needs or expectations and behaviours in different regions based on the functionality provided by these devices. Despite the current penetration of devices, there also remains a huge addressable market. This will translate into the creation of more social customers. New users will join the networks already filled with their friends and families. More social customers join daily and the demand for these devices remains strong.

Table 3—Top five markets by share of global smartphone sales 2011, 2012, and 2016

Country	2011 Market share	2012 Market share	2016 Market share	2011-2016 CAGR
China	18.3%	26.5%	23.0%	26.2%
USA	21.3%	17.8%	14.5%	11.6%
India	2.2%	2.5%	8.5%	57.5%
Brazil	1.8%	2.3%	4.4%	44.0%
United Kingdom	5.3%	4.5%	3.6%	11.5%
Rest of World	51.1%	46.4%	46.0%	18.1%
Source: IDC (Aug 2012)			via: mobiThinking	

In reviewing the data, it was interesting to examine the market share forecast for smartphones. I wondered how many companies were focused on this trend and the need to adjust their organizations to effectively support these customers. Why? As plans are developed, especially for companies with global operations, understanding how the expected shifts will influence investment strategies and customer experience is important. In Table 3, the data shows that the concentration of devices will continue to spread with the dominance of western markets reducing as BRIC (Brazil, Russia, India and China) countries continue their growth rates. In some cases, e.g., Brazil, the expectation is for growth rates four times what is expected in the United States and the United Kingdom. The forecasted rate for India is even higher. That is dramatic growth. However, it is a reflection of current activity in these markets. In BRIC countries, 93 percent of online users are described as "active." Ninety-seven percent of the users in these countries also engage in social networking.[14]

These are trends that the deeply skeptical could take with a dose of salt, and there is room for skeptics. That said, from experience in the telecommunications space in the early days of mobile technology showed the potential speed of acceptance and how it dramatically changes a country. With the infrastructure already in place, the acceptance of smartphones will be a natural extension. It is already happening. While companies make changes to capitalize on the opportunities created by this trend, it is important that they include how they will manage the customer's experience.

> *"It's hard to picture a world without smartphones these days. I mean, we've had them for so long now, and I hardly remember when they were not around. I remember having a **Nokia** phone (not a smartphone) back in the '90s, but that's as far back as I can remember even having the ability to remotely log onto the Internet on a phone. It was when it was still just text on these devices, no images, just pure text. 1993 was the year when the world saw the first real smartphone. It was when the **IBM Simon** was released, and it had minor apps. It had functions such as a fax, a PDA and even a pager. The evolution since then has been nothing less than amazing."*
> —Darell, Richard, *The Evolution of Smartphones* (2012), www. bitrebels.com

Another technology trend that relates to the growth in social media is the increased significance of tablets. As with smartphones, the increase in the number of tablet users has been phenomenal. In the United States, it is estimated that by

2014 there will be approximately 90 million tablet users; there were only 33 million tablet users in 2011.[15] Almost all major electronics manufacturers, including Samsung, Microsoft, Apple, LG, Acer, Blackberry, and others, have tried to find a way to capitalize on the momentum in that sector. As with smartphones, tablet users are also digital natives who have social networking tendencies. More real estate is on these devices' screens and likely more power in the operating systems, more memory and better access to more apps. In a world where mobility is the new "normal," the tablet has joined the smartphone in building platforms on which social customers are being fed. From the trends on smartphones and tablets, we can reasonably conclude that there will be more growth in these segments. This growth equates to more opportunities and more social customers. As long as the need to be "social" remains in its heightened state, methods and strategies applied to reaching and supporting these customers will constantly need attention, review, and possibly revision.

Being public is necessary

With the era of smartphones, tablets, social media, and the social customer comes "publicness."[16] In the same way that individuals have embraced the opportunity to be public, in some cases to the point of being ludicrous, there is growing expectation for companies to behave similarly. Many customers want to be able to relate to companies via their web properties. Some also want to go behind the virtual walls to understand more about what happens within the company and many companies have responded to these demands. The fact that some executives have taken to Twitter, LinkedIn, Facebook, and other social platforms to share with customers is an indication of the acceptance and importance of being part of the social space. Sir Richard Branson, founder of the Virgin Group of companies, is an example of an executive actively involved in social media. His recent count of followers on LinkedIn was near 1.48 million.[17] Does the image of Virgin benefit from his social media participation? Yes, resoundingly so! He clearly embraces the value of sharing in social media, and it is part of the Virgin Group's customer experience strategy. The image he creates in these spaces entices social customers to relate to and purchase from the Virgin brand.

As "publicness" becomes normal, social media forces businesses into a public space. In this space they are searchable, not only because of what they say, but also from what is said about them. The value of effective web presence, "searchability," and responsiveness consequently become more important to companies. It is also important to the social customer who relies on social platforms to find and relate to companies. Companies that accept the value of this "publicness" and act, reap the benefits available in the social customer era. These benefits include ideas from customers, increased customer spending, and referrals from their social customers based on their experiences.

For the companies that find the best ways to adapt and capitalize on the tendency of customers to be social, the issue of benefiting from that loyalty is a factor of significance moving forward. The social customer era is characterized by quick conversions, referrals, and defections. It creates a forum for both osmosis and symbiosis, which previously were separated. Customers can share and be helped in the same instance. An interesting example is how some companies have transformed communities into technical support functions. In the United Kingdom, Giffgaff (www.giffgaff.com), one of their fastest growing telecommunications providers, has established forums where all technical support occurs. The key point to understand here is that customers help customers, all the time. There is a deliberate structure around the strategy that rewards participants and those highly ranked in the community. The fact is the company has invested in trusting the community, whose only common factor is subscribing to Giffgaff, to take care of each other in this way. This is a major shift from the traditional approach of setting up product experts in large call centers with elaborate CRM systems collecting data. Other companies have embraced approaches that subscribe to the multi-channel approach, which includes monitoring social channels and providing responses based on issues raised.

I am not suggesting that either model is more appropriate or necessary. The nature of the products being supported, the customer base, and cost are factors that would be critical to determining the appropriate model to adopt. All approaches, community or multi-channel, which include the active participation of customers, reflect the fact that companies are investing in "trusting" their customers by allowing them to participate in ways they previously wouldn't. That they are part of a social community, where they are inclined to contribute positively to other members, makes it a win-win situation. In applying this trust, companies are also creating fans and allowing them to be ambassadors for areas of the business that traditionally would have been reserved for employees. Social media platforms allow for the broadening of the role of fans because becoming a fan equates to a customer testimonial, which is amplified by social media. Customers are able to broadcast their pleasure and pain, and recommend or reject a company within the same platform.

In the world of social customers, the benefits of the social community are easily extended. Word of mouth has new flavours like "sharing" and "liking." A tweet could transform the fortunes of a business. Imagine a tweet from a superstar about your restaurant, clothing store, or book. This accessibility to a community is a fringe benefit that more customer support strategies are incorporating. It only makes sense to utilize both the trust and knowledge factor that comes with the social customer. While some of the factors, such as trust, would not be new to corporate value systems, their application within a context that encourages extreme flexibility and openness makes the task of managing the customer experience even more difficult. The combination of technologies that allows for constant connection, the power of communities, and the need to extend trust is a challenge companies will need to tackle. There are potentially successful options to deal with this.

In the final analysis, new technology will be introduced to fuel the seemingly insatiable need for people to connect. Who knows what the smartphone or tablet will morph into? With new technology, enterprises will need to continue, if not increase, their focus on social customer characteristics. The social tendency is one of the many characteristics being fuelled by the plethora of mobile devices. And the maturity of the personas will need to be accepted and addressed. Their power as consumers will continue to increase and the likelihood of exuding that power on markets will be high. The fact that more reasons are being found for social networking will prolong the life and value of social media. Attached to that longevity is an increasingly more complex customer persona—the social customer. Success will therefore require increased focus on the traits, tendencies, and idiosyncrasies of this segment of the market, which is already an active majority. The work and role of the customer experience strategist is only going to get more important.

CHAPTER 4
How Social Customers Speak

We would have been considered insane if 20 years ago we were able to envisage and explain a world where a tweet could describe something unlike the sound of a bird or if we predicted that texting would be a popularly used verb. It would hardly have been considered a possibility for people to instantly share videos or that something called a blog would be a source of information and entertainment. The explosion in communications technologies, social media, and the networking revolution has created new words that have corresponding behaviours based on how participants understand the language and intent of the exchanges that occur. In examining the phenomenon of social media on customer experience requirements, it is important to understand how social customers behave and speak.

The social world has brought new vocabulary, with words added daily. What is fascinating is these new words can be infused with existing vocabulary and still be understood by the sender and receiver. In some cases, the structure and grammar defy conventional rules, but users understand each other. Often acronyms are used as they tend to be crisp, cryptic, and concise, for example *LOL, OMG,* and *BTW*.[18] Users tend to mix symbolism (called emoticons) within the structure of sentences and create new terms or symbols organically, which is a normal and expected development.

As people become more engrained in social networking and mobile technologies, they depend increasingly on this vocabulary to optimize the benefits of their interactions. As my teenage daughter explains, "it is faster, direct, and cheaper." While it may be acceptable in informal settings, this method of communication is increasingly being used in the corporate world. This chapter focuses on how social customers speak and the impact of different elements have on developing successful customer experience strategies.

Recently a manager told me about a situation where an employee was not at work due to illness. The employee had notified the manager of the impending absence by text message. The manager was taken aback at the fact that in the eyes of the employee, sending a text message was sufficient notice of absence. Welcome to the age of the Millennials. I understood her chagrin at the fact that short message service (SMS or text messaging) was now considered an acceptable form of business communication, although I am sure the employee sending the text message meant no disrespect. I suppose this is where *LOL* would come in. I advised her to discuss the issue with her team, and consider formally making it an acceptable form of business communication. It should be. After all, banks, telecommunications providers, and other companies send me notices by text message all the time. Many organizations use it as a form of business communication with customers. Why shouldn't we? While the message did get through, which was the core intention, questions about the informal communication method and style of the social customer and the generation driving these methods surfaced.

Outside of the clear clash of generations, there was the absence of both understanding and expectation between the individuals. No doubt the same scenario occurs between companies and their customers. With all the things happening and the millions of transactions, there may not be time or even intent to understand how social customers speak. Companies are challenged to develop methods to decode and respond to the language of the social customer, including meanings often hidden within their vocabulary. Understanding how customers speak, though, opens opportunities for companies to expand service offerings, improve retention, and increase customer experience scores. These are positive outcomes to understanding the basis on which the language and communication style of the social customer is built.

When examined in terms of technology, there is overwhelming data about the major shift in the preferred means of customer communication, and it's happening globally. Verbal communication continues to compete strongly with short messages (SMS) as the core method. Rate plans offered by telecommunications providers globally show a big shift toward data versus voice. A customer may call an organization for information or to resolve an issue, but likely this is different from how he or she connects with family and friends. In the speed of daily life, using text messages and other SMS tools is more commonplace than using voice channels. Commonly, customers prefer using those methods to connect with the companies they do business with. It keeps them within their comfort zone and they remain consistent with the behaviours that made them social customers. That is important, even if it is an unconscious choice. It is not uncommon for customers who just engaged with companies to share their feelings about the experience immediately after as this is part of the social tendency. The social behaviour could start with a tweet, likely followed by sharing on Facebook, and then there may be more feedback later on other social networks. Business leaders looking at these actions must accept that this is a part of how social customers speak. While it may not be considered a conversation or conscious communication, elements within this scenario reflect how social customers speak. Understanding this helps customer experience professionals at all levels develop strategies to effectively communicate with these customers.

The power of tweeters

Social customers use "tweeting" to communicate. Some companies do, too. In the space of 140 characters, Twitter users are able to share, challenge, expose, and impact how others respond.[19] A lot is said via this medium, with more said each year. In 2010 Twitter reported 35 million tweets per day; this has grown to nearly 500 million in 2012.[20] Tweeters are being recognized for the potential impact on the image of a company they are able to have within their networks. *State of the Media: The Social Media Report 2012* provides an interesting picture of how Twitter became a part of "The Global Living Room." They reported that 33 percent of Twitter users tweeted about TV-related content.[21] One could question the relevance of the data and the activity in the context of looking at customer experience strategy. The fact is, these individuals are also customers who likely practice the same tendencies relative to the product or service they are consuming. Social networking behaviour increasingly intersects with consumer behaviour.

Social media has allowed customers to speak publicly on issues and capitalize on the publicity to create pressure on companies to accede to their requests. Depending on the policies adopted by companies, the fear of a tweet or other social media expressions could result in resolutions that would otherwise be different. Social media has driven some companies to increased awareness of the impact of social customer communication. While this often occurs in negative circumstances, the reality is that the social customer is inclined to use the benefits of the social platforms to speak to and about a company. This trait of social customer behaviour forces more companies to accept the need to be truly "public" and adopt elements of publicness within social media environments. This includes proactive declarations on issues, requesting feedback, and in some cases, encouraging co-creation. Increasingly, companies are monitoring social channels to hear what customers are saying and hearing.

For enterprises keen on maintaining or gaining competitive advantage, more focus must be placed on active listening to social customer channels. In the traditional sense, listening was done through surveys, focus groups, or town hall sessions. In the era of the social customer, the concept has widened its meaning and practice. Companies are finding more proactive ways to hear what customers are saying. More programs and tools are being developed to ensure that companies hear and respond. Voice of the customer (VOC) programs, as some are called, are multi-faceted and multi-channel to ensure that all segments of the customer population are being heard. It is important that companies serious about gaining competitive advantage with social customers build these programs. More is required than just building these programs: to extract value, companies must commit to ensuring that they are active and responsive to customer input. A recent study by Cone Communications[22] reported that 46 percent of respondents wanted to receive information and solve problems by social media. However, only 14 percent reported satisfactory experiences based on the online interactions they had. Customer experience programs must ensure that as customers express their opinions through social media on their experience with companies, appropriate methods exist to measure both activity and effectiveness of customer experience strategies. These measures should also be included, at least in the form of a summary, in the company's executive scorecard. Merely counting tweets may provide little value. Finding ways to show the correlation between social customer expressions, a company's proactivity, and overall performance would surely provide valuable information.

Speaking by liking

In the same breath that we accept that a tweet could add spice to your business day or create a messy situation, we should also accept that there are emotional expressions in the language social customers speak. The range of emoticons available is proof. As social customers conduct business, opportunities abound to express the way they feel. While not elaborate, the click of a button now holds great value in determining whether a customer has emotionally invested in a brand or not. Simply put, it is easy to know whether they like a company, product, or change. Or not. Nearly all social media platforms have found their way into most companies' web properties. The trend is to ensure that customers can port themselves across these web spaces seamlessly. This facility allows the customer to speak to companies, relate their experiences, and rate these experiences all in a single session. It is important to some companies that customers indicate their feelings by "liking" on their sites. Many companies are overt and ask that customers "like" them.

United Broke My Guitar

Over 14 million people were provided with a chronicle of Dave Carroll's experience with United Airlines. He reported that his guitar was damaged by United Airlines, for which he requested compensation. His experience did not meet his expectation so he took his experience to social media. The video went viral. United responded and tried to regain some ground by offering more, but the damage was already done. Would this have been the same without an environment where a customer's voice could be sent viral in minutes? I think not. Social media has amplified customer's voices and they speak to, and about, companies and the customer experience they provide. Unfortunately, negative messages tend to find the tailwind to push them far quickly.

As of March 2013 there were 14.4 million views and over 75,000 likes on YouTube for Carroll's video.

This act can be limited to a generic expression or targeted to a product, statement, action, or a myriad of other possibilities. Counting "likes" is a new way, however unscientific, to gauge the sentiment of social customers and the degree to which they choose to speak. For some companies, the "like count" as a percentage of views or visits is a temperature check on the effectiveness of investments that may have been made in a new offering, tool, or process. In the language of marketers, liking is a positive impression. Expressing one's view is useful, and social customers speak that way.

The fact that customers have the option to speak in multiple ways pushes companies to increase their listening capabilities and adjust customer satisfaction measurement strategies, including moving away from periodic, static customer satisfaction surveys to real-time assessment of customer experience. Some examples are social media elements such as "likes," evaluations auto-generated by Customer Relationship Management (CRM) systems, rating systems in forums, and direct surveys conducted by third parties. All these are geared toward hearing more from customers and validating other data already gathered thorough traditional means. More companies have invested in monitoring and responding to comments, questions, and issues raised on social media platforms. This includes the application of products from companies that provide a foray in what is being called social CRM. Products like Jive, Radian 6, Salesforce.com, Yammer, and Lithium have enabled companies to activate their listening and response strategies in more efficent and effective ways. While I would describe the current application of products as early days, an awareness of that customers are speaking in different ways in different places is prudent. Companies should keep their fingers on the pulse of customer sentiments. Early adopters of social CRM are realizing benefits that allow them to know their customers better and enhance their relationships with them. The enhanced relationships lead straight back to the bottom line.

Speaking by spending

While social customers capitalize on the potential of negative comments in social media, they still maintain the power of speaking through their spending power and tendencies. Dollars spent still speak loudly. The global pattern for online transactions remains positive. According to the Boston Consulting Group, the "Internet economy" was worth £121 billion in the United Kingdom in 2010 with a prediction it would reach £221 billion by 2016.[23] This perspective is global. In Australia, PwC reported a steady increase in online spending that stood at US$16 billion in 2012 and predicted it would reach US$27 billion by 2016. In the United States, the online spend in 2011 was US$256 billion. Without stretching these numbers further, we can conclude that the tendency of customers to purchase online remains strong and is increasing. These spending patterns are supported by a profileration of mobile devices, which was previously discussed, that allow social customers to share their views within their networks and shop at will. What may seem like a convoluted set of related equations is merely the social customer at work. Combined with all other related trends such as smartphones, tablets, tweeting, etc., ample evidence exists to show that social customers send messages to companies regularly and in different ways. The spending data also reflects growth in the social customer population. This growth should indicate the need for a corresponding shift in how the customer's experience, strategies, and tools are designed, deployed, and managed. Business success in the era of the social customer will be influenced by the effectiveness of customer experience strategies.

Social media has allowed social customers to say more in so many ways. This has made the language of social customers an invaluable part of their persona and an important component in how businesses look at these customers. Social customers are able to speak in crisp, concise, multi-media ways in a public space with a reasonable expectation of being heard by a significantly broader audience. With this opportunity, social customers can be more direct and confident knowing that the likelihood of reaching their target is enhanced by the power of their networks and the viral effect of social media. Traditional communication methods would not have afforded social customers the same likelihood of engagement, responsiveness, or transparency with companies. The way social customers speak pulls companies into the social sphere. Companies are forced to constantly examine their practices, processes, and offerings to ensure that they are being perceived in a manner that reflects their brand.

CHAPTER 5
Generation Gaps

I walked into work one day and mentioned that I intended to deactivate my Facebook account. While my comment elicited some laughs, the most stirring although somewhat embarrassing response was from Kim, 27, who could not believe that I had an account on Facebook. As far as she was concerned, that would not be something that she would have expected her parents to do, and I was in that category in her eyes. I began to wonder how many other of the under-30 employees felt that way and I conducted a quick poll. It was truly enlightening to realize how differently they saw me, the world, and social media.

As customers become more sophisticated, companies need to develop more intricate strategies to attract their attention and maintain their satisfaction and loyalty. There are many outstanding examples of companies that have invested millions of dollars into managing the needs, nuances, and inclinations of the various generations who admire and consume their products. In the beverage category, Coca-Cola and Pepsi have been giants in that space for many generations and have done numerous things including adding new flavours, new packaging, new advertising, and new products to appeal to the discerning tastes of their customers. The power of a low-carbohydrate, low-calorie product would not likely be the focus of a Baby Boomer who has, in his or her view, seen and done it all. It would be available for the Generation Y professional who is keen to consume products that don't compromise his or her health and wellness goals. The same could be said of companies like Nike or Adidas who are forced to continually innovate to meet the varying requirements of the sophisticated Millennial athlete versus the Baby Boomer who, despite participating in many sports endeavours, was not all that concerned about stress fractures and preventative kinesiology. All companies, at some point and in varying degrees, must acknowledge and cater to the idiosyncrasies of the different generations.

The generation gap is a term popularized in Western countries during the 1960s. It refers to differences between people of a younger generation and their elders, especially between children and parents. Although some generational differences have existed throughout history, modern generation gaps have often been attributed to rapid cultural change in the postmodern period, particularly in matters such as musical tastes, fashion, culture, and politics. Social media is also an interesting element in the discussion of generation gaps.

The way products are developed, how businesses operate, and even how governments develop policies are influenced by their recognition of the different generations. The social era has not changed the need for those involved in managing businesses to acknowledge and plan to address the different requirements of the generations being served. This applies to all aspects of an operation, including customer experience. It would be foolish and counterproductive to design and market a product that successfully attracts the attention of the targeted demographics of the population and not design support structures and processes to meet the needs of that audience. The intricacies applied to plan the product design, sales, and marketing must also apply to the way customers are heard and serviced. A comprehensive customer experience focus would include all these elements. How is that done and what are the keys to ensuring that this attention is applied correctly and in the areas that matter most? Before examining the structure of customer experience models, maybe the question to be addressed initially is what has changed to require this? What is so different about the latest generation?

Numerous studies, dissertations, and other academic works have effectively described the changes that have occurred from the Silent Generation through to the Baby Boomers.[24] Even more information is available for Generation X and Generation Y (the Millennials). With each generation, a matrix of events, inventions, and trends characterize what drove, challenged, and influenced them. It is reasonable to accept that while some factors may be common, for example, the desire for greater economic success, others such as digitization is a feature applicable to only the current generation.

Today a student could stay at home and "read" for a degree, which would have been unthinkable in the 1930s, even though scholarly pursuits were active and in vogue. Members of the Silent Generation who benefitted from tertiary education were counted among society's elite. It was a privilege, and it led to assuming certain roles, both professional and social. Those norms have changed in the world of the Echo Boomers, those of Generation Y, who consider getting a degree a natural extension to their education and in some cases a right. To that extent, huge businesses (online universities, professional designations, etc.) have developed to fulfill those needs. The evolution in that industry remains fascinating, not because IQ is in greater supply but because of the power of the underpinning technology to support easier, faster processes in education. Understandably, the perspective of a Baby Boomer toward tertiary education would be materially different from a Millennial. I have no doubt that when my daughter, currently four years old, gets to the tertiary education stage, she will spend more time on a mobile device completing the requirements to get a degree. Already many educational institutions have graduated to e-books and tablets. The principle of obtaining a degree would remain the same, with similar importance and relevance, but with a very different framework to complete it.

There have been many changes in the economy, politics, technology, and social standards over these generations. Today's comfort with technology was not even a factor influencing the Silent Generation. For them, survival, recovery, and creating social structures dominated an era influenced by wars and a move to industrialization. For the Baby Boomers, the products of their era created both social hope and economic fortune. The foundations created by the Boomers generated wealth and an entrepreneurial framework that made technology an increasingly significant part of economic and social development. The arrival of computers, the Internet, and mobile telephony made the world of the Generation X-ers a dream environment. In the United States in the Clinton era (1993-2001), there would have been very few people who did not embrace the American dream considering the economic buoyancy of that time. [25] This happened in other regions as well. The economic performance and success of the Asian tigers (Taiwan, South Korea, Hong Kong, and Singapore) is something I vividly remember being discussed frequently in developing countries. At the same time, new technologies came rushing in, solidifying the views about the possibility of economic nirvana. Buzz words and management practices also abound to ensure that enterprises kept pace with the perceived requirements to succeed. Whether it was the focus on quality and the application of Total Quality Management (TQM) or the introduction of computer networks run on mainframes, management practices across the generations were distinctly different. While this picture may have different hues based on specific circumstances, all countries experienced social, political, and economic differences between the generations.

Accepting that there were real differences between the generations, we also should realize that the advent of social media has created a layer of equalization between generations as all of them participate in social networking and derive benefits from it. In looking at these actions across the different generations, important issues come to light that business leaders should examine. One is how to manage customer experience across the generations using social platforms. If the goal is to derive revenue from each generation in the different markets, it is also crucial to determine how best they will be supported across the customer experience cycle. While the behaviour of social customers of different generations is similar, the fact is they are from different generations. Understanding how to focus solutions to meet these different needs as part of a customer experience strategy is important. In this chapter, we will focus on Millennials because the pulse of social media revolves around them, their needs, and tendencies. I would argue that they have the greatest effect currently on how markets, products, and all activities correlated to both are being shaped. While the generation that I describe as M2, for those born after the year 2000 (Y2K), will have an impact as well, the framework being set by Millennials is likely to be extended by the new generation versus the revolution that is currently in full flow.

The body of work related to Millennials is extensive. In a report done by Myers and Sadaghaini, they described Millennials in the workplace as impatient, self-assured, exposed, socially-conscious, sheltered, and a range of other adjectives based on the socio-economic experiences of the last two decades. [26] The view is that the period of relatively stable socio-economic circumstances, coupled with advances in technology have created entrants to the workforce that are driven by very different things. The need for work-life balance, flexibility, increased communication, and current technology were listed as key to the ideal work circumstance for these workers. The report further outlined their acceptance of virtual working arrangements, affirmative communication, technology mediated communication, and rapid career progression as other features of the world in which they prefer to work. It is therefore not surprising that when these individuals switch to their roles as customers, some of the same traits, behaviours, and expectations transition with them. The fact that they are digital natives leads to an acceptance of a chat option, or a webbot, as preferred methods for receiving support, while understandably a Baby Boomer may prefer to complete the same transaction face-to-face or by telephone. [27]

I don't intend to cast a net over all people of a particular generation as I accept that each person is different. That said, some things, once started in a particular time or circumstance, result in comfort to those for whom it was commonplace. An example would be the comfort and acceptance Baby Boomers had with cars without air conditioning. No one in today's generation (M2) would consider it an optional feature. I can imagine my kids whining endlessly about the discomfort. The reality is, people are more comfortable in situations they are used to or can easily relate to. Where change is required, the degree to which it is accepted will be influenced by the added comfort, value, or proposed benefit relative to the former situation. The rate of acceptance of social media, its benefits, and potential value would therefore be different across the generations since some were born into it while others had to be trained.

Recently, a friend of mine proudly declared how active her mother, who was nearing 70, was on Facebook and Twitter. Her mother was a management consultant for many years. Despite initial reluctance, she learned to accept the power of social networking technologies and adjusted from what she knew growing up so she could benefit from the new trends. She did many things online and became a social customer. Others in her generation are still limited to using the Internet for email and information gathering only. They may be very satisfied with using the technologies in those ways. Similarly, some people born in the heart of the social networking revolution are not drawn to the technologies and associated behaviours as much as others. In either case, that is a reality business leaders grapple with as they determine how best to support and get optimum value from the relationships with these customers.

The proliferation of social technologies has created a generation with a broader appreciation of globalization. Even where tools and methods are traditional, there is greater acceptance of global relationships and the value they bring. It is not uncommon for companies to have roles where there is direct interaction between people geographically dispersed and culturally different. For people in those roles, life is made easier by the fact that the connections they maintain through social platforms outside of work are similar. Sharing pictures or other personal details and events with friends and family are invariably virtual and normal.

This "normal" also translates into consumption patterns. A while ago some team members asked me to join their shopping club. They ordered products (knock-offs, I think) from an online distribution club based in China. Yes, China. We were in Canada. It was suggested without a blink at the thought of the inherent risks in virtual transactions. That said, I was thinking like a Gen-Xer who, while open to virtual transactions, had more boundaries than my Millennial colleagues. In their world, the globe was the market. Consumption, bargains, and all the other elements involved with commerce were not limited by physical constraints. They were right. Everything was done online and the limits were pushed further in all sectors. They may have been graduates of online courses or have dated online; the fact is they were digital natives who were not accustomed to technological restraints. As customers, they were even more pragmatic.

Workplaces have responded to the impact of this gregarious generation with many interesting strategies employed. Without the intervention of the labour movement, as was the case for the Boomers and Gen-Xers, there have been positive responses to the fact that attracting and retaining Millennials requires a different approach. Some companies, as listed below, have offered perks and implemented initiatives in direct response to the impact of Millennials,[28] including

- Google—flexible work hours and expectations, e.g., free personal time during the workday
- Qualcomm—on-site farmers market
- PCL Construction—unlimited sick days
- Umpqua Bank—loans for business attire
- DPR Construction—$20k for referrals

The list is by no means exhaustive of the many workplace initiatives in response to the needs of the new generation. The parallel is that similar if not greater approaches must also be applied to deal with these same workers in their "customer" persona.

The last factors I want to examine regarding the distinction between the generations are loyalty and patience. The fact that broadband is a feature in many households, especially in developed economies, has allowed Millennials to apply a different perspective on "slow." For those who, like me, experienced dial-up Internet connections, the fuss triggered by a lack of 3G coverage is humorous. However, it is understandable since it is unfathomable for the generation born into social technologies. Speed and constant access to connectivity has reduced tolerance levels. It has also opened up more options around the use of time since much more can be done in less time. People expect to achieve more with their time and waiting on others does not achieve that. This impatience also translates in their likelihood to be less loyal, or perceived that way, compared to Boomers or Gen-Xers. The tendency is to change jobs more often or satisfy personal inclinations such as world travel, volunteering, or social activism versus sticking it out with an employer. I use these examples because when the customer persona is examined, the same traits are seen. It is not surprising, therefore, that some traditional loyalty programs may not appeal as strongly to Millennials. Consequently, new marketing approaches have been developed to attract and promote loyalty with this generation, while accepting the transient nature of their relationships.

The era of the social customer does minimize, if not eliminate in some cases, the differences in the generations. The technologies equalize all users and, to a degree, make the task of customer experience professionals a little easier. In the social networking realm, transformation is readily facilitated and the tools and options cater to everyone. Some people are still not sold on the value or benefits of the social networking world and remain satisfied with traditional methods. Those customers' needs must also be considered and their experience is also important. People responsible for building strategy must have a good understanding of the customer base profile and structure processes that cater to them. In many cases, the degree to which customers change will be influenced by how much disruption occurs to activities that were common to their generation. For Millennials, a bank closing a branch to reduce operating costs may mean little since they mainly use automated tellers and online tools. Another generation may find that change more disturbing. Not that they would prevent it, but they may, at increased cost to themselves, maintain the old practice instead of learning a new method. Social customers, despite the generation they belong to, will likely accept changes that fit their behaviour. In many cases, they encourage these changes and where the changes do not fit their preferences, they raise their voices through social platforms. Many companies in recent times have been challenged and have reversed changes based on feedback on social channels, which is a good thing.

CHAPTER 6
Social Customers Equals Higher Expectations

In September 2012, I attended the annual conference hosted by Salesforce.com in San Francisco. Dreamforce, as the conference is called, attracted a record number of registrants; in excess of 90,000 people. The event was fantastic with numerous sessions focussed on using technology, albeit related to the offerings from Salesforce.com and its partners, to improve the quality of customer interactions and business processes. In one session, Anthony (Tony) Robbins, an American self-help author and motivational speaker, presented his usual high-octane material to a packed audience. A few things stood out to me. First, almost everyone, had a smartphone or iPad capturing material from the giant screens in the conference hall. Second, the screen had a constant stream of tweets from audience members who were sharing, real-time, what was being said (as much as 140 characters allowed). As I watched these dynamics, I was overwhelmed, but also excited about how technology changes allowed thousands of people to facilitate the needs and wants of their customers and contacts with speed, effectiveness, and simplicity. I also thought about the many changes companies had to make to delight customers in an era where technology is as pervasive as ours.

When the Internet was developed in the 1960s, expectations were rather simple: connect computers over distance and share information. Success! As the world gravitated toward the Internet and started to optimize it, the possibilities began to broaden and more needs were satisfied by using the available protocols to deliver services that were previously done through direct contact. With time it became necessary to have a website, and that website became the face of an organization. Using the Internet reflected awareness and acceptance of the power and influence of the worldwide web. Those who developed the Internet may not have envisaged it growing to billions of users. They also may not have imagined that it would be the driving force behind the creation of many industries and contribute to the livelihood of millions of people daily all over the world. It has moved significantly past its initial design.

Internet use has become interactive and varied and will continue to evolve. Merely using it in a mode where pages are static and connected by simple hyperlinks is unacceptable, if not prehistoric. It would be tantamount to suggesting that someone purchase a smartphone with the primary purpose of making phone calls. Who does that? No one, unless one chooses to resist the power of the technologies. I find it hilarious when I see someone pull out a regular flip-phone to make or receive a call. My initial instinct is to wonder how the person sends text messages using that device. The tendency is to expect everyone to be part of the social networking revolution and therefore have devices that reflect that since that is where the world is at. Views differ on whether the convergence of technologies, which drives the world of social media, is a good or bad thing. It's a debatable issue! Nevertheless, it is here to stay and it proliferates at an astonishing pace.

Have you ever taken the time to watch people who are addicted to their mobile devices? They are everywhere: on the streets, in public transportation, in the office, and even behind steering wheels. They frequently use or check their phones. A few seconds go by and they check again. Really! Understandably, distracted driving regulations are being imposed in many places. In August 2012, I was travelling on the underground train in London when the reality of my times hit me, again! Ten people were sitting in the section where I was, with an equal gender distribution. Of the 10 people, 6 used their mobile phones (all smartphones), 1 read a magazine and another did a crossword puzzle while 2 others did nothing. The oldest of the group, who appeared to be over 50 years, read a magazine. It looked like people using their mobile devices were on social media. I think it's likely that there was no urgency for the people using mobile devices. After all, getting adequate signals on those trains is limited. Likely the majority of users were capitalizing on the short window available to catch up on Facebook and Twitter, to ensure that they stayed current and responded instantly. If they didn't, there may be anxiety and then desire to catch up when enough signal and bandwidth become available. This happens daily all over the world and the proliferation of devices that facilitate easy access and interconnectedness will continue to drive this behaviour.

Why are the changes in customer attitudes an issue when looking at customer experience? How is it relevant to what this book is about? In previous chapters, I discussed social media, different generational traits and the dynamics involved, including the growth of mobile technology. The use and demands of social media have produced characteristics in consumers that are critical to understand to develop appropriate support mechanisms. As their expectations of the technologies change, so do their expectations of the companies. In the same way that they are expected to adjust their consumption and transaction patterns, similarly they look for changes to occur from those marketing, selling, and supporting these goods and services. To be successful, companies must adapt the structure of service and support options to fulfill the needs of the evolving customer profiles. This begins with understanding the customer experience cycle and applying solutions in each phase to deliver the desired experience for these customers.

According to Forrester's *Global Social Media Adoption* report, there is continued, steady growth in the number of active users of social media in all regions of the globe, which influences Internet use in many areas.[29] Shopping, banking, games, gambling, pornography, publishing, and other Internet services keep users coming back. Thirty percent of the world's population were Internet users in 2010, which is an increase of more than 400 percent over the seven percent in 2001.[30] In most cases, the products are getting cheaper, better, and offer real-time options that make it understandable that consumers would return. An example would be a consumer who starts online banking because it saves time and money and minimizes the need to go to a branch. Over time, the consumer would think that no branches are available and seek resolutions through the virtual media. The same applies to shopping online, where the same medium provides options to get questions answered similar to how it facilitated the search, review, and purchase of the good or service. These examples spread into many other areas. Customers who purchase airline tickets online will likely check in online for their flight.

The availability of these options has raised the base standard for providing services. With the advent of automated teller machines (ATM), customers don't need to visit a branch to withdraw money. A commercial bank that does not offer such options would be considered pre-modern. With the growth in web services, mobile computing, and social platforms, having an app for mobile banking on multiple operating systems and devices is considered basic as it allows customers to bank on demand. Boundaries continue to be pushed as customers redefine the concepts of instant requirements. Wants have become needs with degrees of urgency around them.

Companies are expected to aspire to minimum global standards, especially with the increased global penetration of Internet access and broadband. The customer's view is that almost all services should be universal, with mobile phones working wherever they roam, access to bank accounts, and the ability to transact business as they move from place to place. The mere desire to do all these things reflects the customer's growing expectation and perspective on urgency. Companies are pushed to respond to the customer's perspective to maintain competitive advantage. Being able to match the customer's perspective of urgent could be material. Do you ever send quotation requests to companies? How often does the first to respond gain the upper hand? The processes that attracted these consumers, in many cases, provided incentives and reflected an understanding of the value of staying current and connected. Banks give the impression that you can always access your money, telecommunications providers rave about their network, and many companies promote their ability to keep their customers up-to-date. Understandably, customers' expectations continue to rise, with the desire to have their expectation realized if not exceeded.

Good reasons exist for higher customer expectations. With the power of the technologies available, customers question limitations. The power of the web means customers expect to access services 24/7/365. If I travel from North America to Asia, time zone differences are a non-issue in my mind. There should be no disruption to accessing my bank account, paying bills online, or transferring data between systems. While there may be no degree of urgency to my requests, my expectation is built on the fact that instant account access or changes are normal activities. It is no different than expecting a McDonald's restaurant in any part of the world to provide a quick meal at a reasonable cost that can be super-sized. Why would anything be different whether I am in Barcelona, Bangalore, or Baltimore? For the social customer who is often connected, technologies that facilitate constant social connections are also available to businesses. Therefore, understandably customers have raised their standards for service as most things are considered urgent so systems and processes should be in place to deliver instant results.

A big driver in all this is the fact that Millennial customers are pushing the boundaries on what technologies can do in different forums. As digital natives, they are so experienced with technologies that it is normal to push for more. A recent report by eMarketer.com and comscore.com showed that consumers aged 18-34 years were likely to use their mobile devices and tablets to complete greater than 50 percent of their online purchases. As Graph 3 shows, consumers aged 35-54 were at an average of 36 percent.[31]

Graph 3—Users making online purchases by age and device

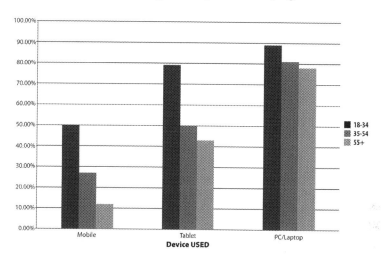

Source: *Why Tablet Users are a Retailers Dream*—eMarketer.com (2012)

The ability to act on these desires through the different options and via mobile tools encourages impulse purchasing. The fact that increasingly more time is being spent on these devices, coupled with aggressive marketing, increases the adrenalin associated with consumption. Unsurprisingly, online spending in the United States topped US$256 billion in 2011. The largest proportion of this was for retail purchases that stood at US$162 billion. As Table 4 shows, despite economic challenges in the United States, the wave of being online and completing transactions continue to grow. The growth in social customers is reflected in the increased online spending.

Table 4—US online consumer spending by categories ($ billion U.S.)

Category	2010	2011
Books	1.0	1.1
Travel	85.2	94.0
Retail	142.5	162.0

Source: comscore.com

In many ways, the wave of online activity, expectations, and challenges to businesses is led by the Millennial generation. They continue to push standards for speed. In their world, technology helps deliver on their expectations and companies are obligated to find ways to make this happen. In this era a customer can purchase products using a mobile phone, design a house using an iPad, or pay for coffee by scanning a QR code, so expecting speed is standard. For some, success is now defined by the speed at which customers can complete their activity.

In the face of that fact, there must be focus on how these needs can be managed to deliver a satisfying customer experience. It will not always be possible to meet the urgent needs of the customer so a reasonable compromise will need to be reached, which could take many forms. In some industries, Interactive Voice Response systems (IVRs) provide callback options as a compromise to not being able to accept a live voice interaction in a short period of time. In Canada, Ally bank added a call wait time notification on its website. Should customers—who are already in self-serve mode—choose to call, they know what to expect. This is in addition to multi-channel support options (voice, email, and chat). This good feature acknowledges the customer's value and promises to act. That said, increasingly more customers are demanding quicker resolutions that will push companies to invest in more solutions, which allow customers to resolve issues on their own, faster, with less hassle.

Having said all this, what are owners of the strategy for customer experience going to do to ensure that their organization remains competitive? The first is to realize that expecting speed is real. The premium on time cannot be overstated and therefore the principles of customer support strategies must be built on easy, speedy resolutions. To achieve this, many company operations must systematically focus on their impact on customer experience. It is not something deferred to the customer service team. All phases of the customer experience cycle should reflect the value of meeting customer's expectations for speed as this has value on a company's bottom line. In another chapter we will speak about tools and techniques related to the actual interaction.

Another factor to consider while building solutions in response to the demands for urgency is that other generations are seeing the impact Millennials are having and they are adjusting their tolerance thresholds. There may not be a similar premium on speed, but they are also raising the standards for how they expect to be treated. With that in mind, the focus on multi-channel support strategies remains in vogue. However, the functionality of these channels may need to be refreshed or changed entirely. This could include ensuring integration of the different support channels. Independent customer applications should be integrated. The same applies to the way teams work inside many companies. Independent customer-centricity does not produce optimal results, but reflects immaturity in customer experience management.

While building strategies to counter the eternal urgency social customers demand, businesses also need to operate in a responsible, successful manner. Generating shareholder value, creating wealth for partners, and supporting the employees' livelihood remains important. Responding to customers need for urgency can deliver positive returns. Many reports and case studies show positive returns from addressing customer needs. A good example is the positive growth of Starbucks.[32] Understanding the need for speed and connectivity, an investment in free Wi-Fi has resulted in customers spending more time and money on their premium products. I am guilty of doing it. Other things would have contributed to the overall success of the company, but their understanding, acknowledgement, and response to the traits of the generations of customers who require "instant and urgent" is a big factor. Starbucks CEO Howard Schultz stated in *Fortune* magazine (December 2011) that the company was not in the coffee business but in the "experience" business.[33] Starbucks has focussed on being customers' "third home." The décor, furniture, music, and free Wi-Fi are all part of a comprehensive strategy to create a customer experience that engages, satisfies, and keeps them coming back. Not surprisingly, more companies are finding ways to respond to their understanding of these new types of customers. Airlines have ventured into offering in-flight Internet access to augment their entertainment systems. Financial services companies provide mobile access on all platforms (iOS or Android) to customers' accounts. The responses to "instant and urgent" are being built to be location and technology agnostic, meaning customers can increasingly expect global standards and consistent experiences no matter where they're located or how they engage.

The social customer's demands will continue to increase. In many cases merely because they can. This could be perceived as pressure on companies and an unfair advantage for customers. It could also be perceived as an opportunity for growth. Companies that develop systematic methods to deliver on customer demands will create differentiation in sectors where there is little to distinguish providers. The customer perceives such organizations as responsive, nimble, and forward-thinking. Ultimately it feeds customer loyalty, which delivers financial benefits. As technology creates opportunities, customers will have the power to move faster, which leads to higher expectations. Companies are challenged to capitalize on the opportunities provided by social technologies to respond to the urgency that the social customers see as normal. Responding positively has benefits.

CHAPTER 7
Getting the Social Customer to Stay

With all the activity on social networks, with new products, features, and services being released, getting social customers to stay with a brand or product requires constant focus. In a landscape that facilitates relatively easy access and defection, increased investment is being made to understand the correct approaches to get social customers to stay. For some organizations it is much harder than others, although we can surmise that all companies travel the same road. Facebook has been able to attract over one billion registered users, while Pinterest is still working toward its first 100 million. Who knows where they will both end up? What is clear is that their success, as does that of all businesses, will be built on the degree to which they are able to encourage customer loyalty to their products and brand. In the world of social networking, this loyalty extends to applying the features of social media for the benefit of everyone. Strategies that were applied to customers prior to the era of the social customer, while still important in some segments, are not universally applicable to the social customer. New, integrated approaches to achieving this "stickiness" are required. The role of customer experience professionals is an important part of this process.

In this chapter, I want to apply a different perspective to the issue of customer loyalty. It is based on the integral role customer experience and the accompanying support strategies play in achieving customer loyalty. Many discussions around customer loyalty are viewed from the marketing perspective and the tactics applied through various programs to entice customers. All those elements are important and will remain critical to corporate strategy. For those who focus on building relationships after the initial sales cycle is completed, other elements must be perfected for the organization to prolong the value of the customer and extract the returns from investment in previous phases of the customers' life cycle with the company. Getting the customer to stay has very tangible benefits: the most logical is the revenue potential. Customers who have become attached to a brand are likely to spend more, be less susceptible to competitive pressures, be likely to recommend, and are also more likely to be understanding and forgiving. These outcomes are all important in different ways and as companies devise support strategies, they should include them in their customer experience solutions, starting with the customer experience strategy.

Social networking has allowed customers to do more, including sharing similar interests with others. In building strategies to support social customers, more is being done to facilitate sharing. Doing so creates an opportunity for customers to learn more about products and services, while at the same time engage in an activity that is a normal part of social networking. Based on the facts discussed in previous chapters about the growth in mobile devices and tablets, social sharing will increase. This increased use creates an opportunity to move customers through loyalty phases to create advocacy and referral. One way to get social customers to stay is to convert them into advocates. This is done in a number of ways, including using them as part of the support framework.

For many years technology companies have facilitated forums to allow users to share information and solutions. In the social networking era, companies include support forums as part of their web properties so customers can assist other customers to solve product problems. In an effort to show gratitude and promote the role customers play in their support strategies, some companies have included elements of recognition and reward in their forums. Rating systems (based on number of posts, etc.), member categories (e.g. Guru, Super-user, etc.), and loyalty points have been implemented to encourage customers helping customers. I am inclined to rate vacation spots and restaurants primarily to help others. I also find it encouraging to see my "star count" after each review submitted. It gives me a sense of value and suggests that the organization and those seeing my reviews appreciate my effort. These methods of customer recognition are managed through the integration and increased capabilities of CRM systems and by adding social elements, e.g., like, share, and email to friend options, to these systems

So Easy to Trust Friends

Our family has been a Honda customer for many years. Recently we lost a car through an accident and began looking at a new Honda, until a chat with our neighbour opened a new possibility. He was a Honda customer who had bought a new Hyundai and raved about it. He said the ratings on this new car were as good, in some cases better, than his Honda. Most of his initial review came from friends on social media. He was enjoying his new car and had no hard feelings about Honda; it was just that he had found a better deal based on what his network had to say. Guess what? Our replacement was not a Honda.

Trust is important

Effective customer experience strategies include knowing and understanding one's customers. Having gotten to know them, the critical element of trust must be fostered to build the relationship, establish loyalty, and thereafter transition to higher levels of loyalty. Trust is important. The concept of trust in what is a virtual relationship may sometimes appear exaggerated and in some cases it may be. However, in the context of the relationship established between a social customer and a supplier of goods and services, it is an extremely important part of the equation. Brands have developed great reputations through online transactions and interactions. There have been no phone calls, no customer forums, no open days, or any other opportunity for those involved to put names to faces. Yet trillions of dollars move from wallets to accounts as products are consumed. As this happens, the trust factor determines the degree to which those brands grow or fade. Trust applies to descriptions on a website, the application of terms and conditions, responses to queries, the quality of products on arrival, and also the effectiveness, including honesty, of the support processes, should they be needed.

Online retailers (etailers) continue to do strong business globally. An element that facilitates that is the trust that they have established with their customers. If I order a product from Zappos, Beyond the Rack, or Amazon, my experience will be influenced by the efficiency of that transaction. Great care needs to go into the details related to online presence and the associated interactions. The collective impact of the different parts results in the desired experience and ultimate degree of loyalty. This includes ensuring that support organizations reflect and practice the brand elements conveyed to the social customer.

Recently, as our family planned our annual vacation, we compared packages on different travel sites. Our preferred choice of rooms was only available on one site, even though we wanted the options and price from another site. To explore the possibility of getting all we wanted in one place, we called their support centre to ask questions. The experience was so deflating that we decided to purchase from another site. We spent several thousand dollars and our customer experience rating meter slipped to zero for that brand. We had shopped there before without needing to contact them, however our first support interaction erased our trust. We are unlikely to buy from them again and we would not recommend them. The loyalty seed was killed, influenced by the support experience. We defected and no one knew.

It could be argued that we had no reason to be loyal, which would be fair. However, I would suggest that all organizations want repeat business and are keen to build trust with customers.

To achieve that, business leaders must ensure that their strategy to get social customers to be sticky includes alignment of support options with all other parts of the customer journey. For the customer to trust the brand, all parts of the process should earn that trust.

In addition to the element of trust, successful customer experience models must integrate the environment in which social customers are comfortable. Increasingly, companies are creating communities within their web properties to facilitate interaction between customers. In the process, systems are in place to understand the behaviour and contribution of different members and recognize them. The concept of "super fans" is standard in social networking language and more companies are trying to find ways to create and maintain super fans. The role of these customers ranges widely depending on the environment, but they can become key resources within these communities, to other customers, and in many cases to the company and the brand. This process moves the customer from merely "liking" the company to putting themselves and their reputations on the line in support of the company. That is loyalty. Many customer support forums are completely customer driven, with the expertise coming from the users, who often are well-versed with the product or have valuable opinions and insights that solve issues others have. While the concept of support forums is by no means novel, establishing and facilitating them within the virtual walls of corporate web properties is still fairly new. Active customer participation is a solution to drive loyalty with social customers.

Another basic component to driving stickiness with the social customer is to deliver excellent service within the spaces that they frequent. Businesses need to invest in the appropriate technology that would allow for efficient, friendly tools to support these customers. Recently, more companies are offering multi-channel support that includes mobile apps, SMS, and social media, which is in addition to the basic voice, email, and chat options. Others have surged further by incorporating support into social portals that provides more options to engage with a company. The realm of supporting the customer will be discussed in greater detail in the next chapter on customer service 2.0. The idea being highlighted here is that as part of the strategy to deliver fantastic customer experiences there must be a fusion between the marketing, sales, and support plans to build on the trust ascribed to the company's brand. Those charged with delivering or supporting these experiences must understand this fusion and operate in a manner that reflects this understanding.

One of the big benefits of the social world and the social customer is the dissolution of barriers between people of common interest or traits. With social media, consumers are now able to speak freely and honestly within their social circles. Their loyalty can be shared with others. Companies that want to have customers become loyal fans are therefore challenged to reduce many of the mechanisms that previously restricted candid, honest dialogue or resolution of issues. The super-fan, while not always overcome with unbounded curiosity, will in many cases challenge decisions, ideas, or other output from a company in the interest of the customer community. This behaviour needs to be understood and accepted, and not in a confrontational manner or by wielding power. Many companies have, as part of their customer experience programs, established customer advocacy roles or customer feedback boards that allow for insight from customers. This positively serves the interests of both the customer and the company. The experience of cosmetic company Sephora[34]is well documented and cited to demonstrate the value of honest engagement to create and sustain customer loyalty. Their Beauty Insider program does more than just reward customers for spending. The program is tied back to the impact it has on their bottom line results. Through effective execution, they are able to report material differences in the spending patterns of "Insiders." They buy more and the program allows participants to get to different levels of importance. I am sure the model is not sinister or aggressive but through the engagement and trust that develops, the consumer feels no reservation to acquiring more products. This example shows that positive benefits can be derived from implementing ideas using social platforms based on an increased sense of loyalty and trust. Goodwill and social capital translate into more revenue.

Facilitating customer feedback is also an important element in using customer experience investment to drive customer loyalty. In the social customer era, customers have lots to say. In volunteering opinions as much as the social customer is inclined to, the expectation is that their opinion should matter. Recently the Swing Group reported that 34 percent of bloggers posted about a product or brand.[35] While we could argue that most of what was said could be construed as negative, it is also fair to counter that so much more is said that does not get to the attention of those monitoring the social airwaves. In cases where the views of customers are received, directly or indirectly, there is great value in recognizing and responding to them. It gives credibility to the brand and its promises and disarms and resets the customer in terms of how they perceive both the organization's product and brand. A potential loss of a customer could be transformed into a raving fan through acknowledgement and responsiveness. In some cases, companies may need to change their stance or policies as the light of public scrutiny gets applied. Being seen as an organization that is flexible and honest based on customer feedback contributes to customers being more loyal. In an earlier chapter we discussed "publicness" and its role in the era of the social customer. Loyalty is impacted by the extent to which organizations choose to be transparent with their customers. While there is no single prescription to recommend for these circumstances, it is important to have processes that encourage and facilitate these exchanges.

The benefits that companies derive from customer loyalty are understood, usually in terms of revenue metrics. Billions are invested in programs each year to achieve this. However, with the social customer significantly more can be achieved and this should be captured in customer experience strategies. The power of the loyal social customer is exponentially greater than in previous generations. We could apply Metcalfe's Law to this situation, even though it is somewhat technical.[36] The fact is social customers have a strong multiplier effect that can be positively exploited.

Social customers, as do all customers, desire experiences that are pleasant, fast, and valuable. What is significantly different is that the service they desire can be delivered within the social platform that they frequent at a lower cost than traditional means. Even more effective is designing solutions that allow customers to solve issues on their own. Not only would it be quicker, but it also demonstrates an understanding of the social customer and a systematic approach to designing processes to support them. Applying discipline in early stages of the customer experience cycle results in clearer processes. This reduces handle times and makes corrective solutions more effective. Have you ever wondered how much it costs some companies to solve the problem you raised with them? Recently it took me eight interactions to have a refund processed by a company that billed me incorrectly. The resolution process cost way more than the problem, and my likelihood to purchase or recommend eroded with each interaction. I am sure that company had no customer experience strategy.

As companies work to get social customers to become and stay loyal, many have included a measure of the customers' likelihood to recommend (Net Promoter Score) as part of their measure of success. It is important to know not only how customers feel about their experience, but also whether they are likely to share that experience. The social customer has the ability to quickly act on those inclinations. Ultimately, the degree of loyalty shown by social customers will be a function of the effectiveness of the engagement between them and the company. The solutions implemented to promote stickiness should include how success will be ultimately measured. The goal should be to have all phases of the customer experience cycle include elements that foster loyalty. It provides a broader foundation on which the customer's experience is built, reflects a clear strategy, and is more likely to achieve the organization's desired outcomes.

Chapter 8
Customer Service 2.0

It is easy to get sucked into the hype of new technologies, academic prognostications, or recent events. The power of the web, social media, and all its derivatives are so pervasive, it is easy to think the world has forgotten traditional means of living and is entirely driven by bits and bytes. In putting this book together, I tried to maintain a reasonable sense of what happens in businesses daily. However, the fact remains that major changes have occurred and will continue as convergence of the digital and social eras morph our society and businesses. As this evolution continues, the heightened focus on customers will continue to change the way customers are acquired and ultimately supported. My concept of customer service 2.0 is an extrapolation of the concepts around the evolution of social media and the application of a matching support framework to mirror the changes in markets, customers, and everything in between. It is the optimization of social media and other methods to deliver positive experiences to social customers.

Customer service 2.0 is sometimes referred to as "social care." Other extensions to the concept acknowledge the need to do more in response to heightened customer expectations. A recent study by NM Incite revealed that greater than half of social media users sought customer service via social channels.[37] It also cited the expectation of prompt response (same day) through those channels. The solution to these expectations is to have social platforms integrated in support offerings despite known risks. Social customers have the benefit of being able to assess and quickly comment on the support received. Word spreads quickly depending on the source, which is a significant change.

Previously, a customer would try to resolve issues by going to the customer service agent. Should the issue not get resolved, the next step would be to climb the chain of command of the company. Not anymore. The new option is to tweet or post. The potential of a viral, social utterance, in some cases, has infinite value. The risk versus reward impacts in this environment can be scary. In some cases, it challenges organizations to invest more in processes and people to ensure the risks are clearly understood and mitigated. It is also important to ensure that the benefits are optimized fully. With the steady increase in the number of social customers who opt to use social customer support options, failure to mitigate risks and optimize benefits can materially impact the overall performance of the company.

As we discussed in earlier chapters, significant traffic is on the Web including trillions of dollars of consumer purchases. As economic activity continues, service and support for the products being sold are needed. While most customers would prefer never to have an issue with a product, they also accept that defects occur. These could be incredibly simple, such as changing a setting on an application, or super complex, requiring return, repair, or replacement. Most important is effective resolution. Whatever the extent of the requirement for resolution, companies, whether directly or through an agent, are expected to provide some mechanism to deal expeditiously with the inevitable. These expectations vary, and this is where business leaders and customer experience professionals may need to make the greatest adjustments. This occurs because expectations regarding service and support are becoming aligned to transaction methods. The characteristics and features of the transaction process are the standard by which the support processes are being evaluated. In a world where nearly everything can be bought through the Web, the corresponding expectation is that almost all things can be resolved in the same way. Is this reasonable? Maybe.

The new era of customer service requires several key elements to ensure an effective foundation on which to deliver on customers' expectations and provide competitive advantage for organizations. Different models guide organizations on the best approach to take in designing and implementing solutions to support customers. In my opinion, each model comes back to a simple framework that includes three core elements. These elements intersect in different ways based on the overall focus, investment appetite, and leadership of an organization. The figure below depicts these:

Figure 1: Elements of support models for customer service 2.0

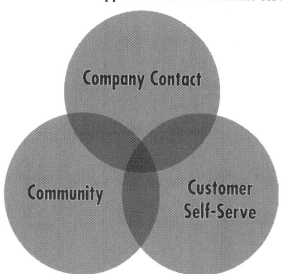

Offerings within Company Contact enable customers to get assistance from support organizations (direct or indirect). These include traditional contact center offerings of voice, chat, email, or other similar methods. As customers expect improved offerings, there are interesting developments within the contact centre to satisfy the social customer. These include more intelligent interactive voice response (IVR) systems that carry service messages, advisories, and in some cases frequently asked questions (FAQs). Chat tools have expanded to facilitate remote collaboration. Customer Relationship Management (CRM) systems have continuously improved with most offering standard options that allow for integration within the social world. Support agents commonly push information to customers through their social profile.

Another popular part of customer service 2.0 is SMS. It is often used to collect and respond to customer queries. These tools integrate with an already converged telephony and service management tool to maintain correlation to the customer data. Contact centres have become hubs of correlated channels managing multiple sources of inputs and outputs as they try to enhance their service offering to the social customer. There remains an active population of customers who will still resort initially to getting help by contacting companies directly.

The model also references elements that allow customers to find support on their own through company-provided properties. These include product manuals, online knowledge bases, or other tools designed to allow customers autonomy in defining their issue and finding answers. Increasingly, technologies that simulate interactions with a contact centre are being integrated into customer self-serve portals. Having intelligence within these tools increases the likelihood of customers resolving their issues quickly. Webbots, videos, simulators, and other technologies have become part of self-service options. Companies investing in these tools are increasing the chances of call deflection and heightening the user experience. These tools are integrated into web properties and are available on mobile devices. It is increasingly standard to log and resolve support issues with a tablet or smartphone. Even grocery stores have found value in having express cashiers and self-checkout lines. These options continue to evolve with the new experiment involving checking out using a smartphone that scans QR codes. Broadening the scope of self-serve options is validation that companies are being pulled by the socially mobile practices of their customers. My cable provider allows me to control my personal video recorder (PVR) from my smartphone. Even the printer in my home office has that feature.

The element of forming a community around a product is the latest option and is more directly aligned to the social customer than all the others. Allowing customers to share issues and solutions within a forum goes to the heart of optimizing social media platforms and practices to provide customer service 2.0. It facilitates increased understanding and expertise on the product within the community (as opposed to within the manufacturer or agent), and allows customers to become true experts and advocates of products. Through these communities, companies are able to significantly reduce their support costs and increase the speed and scope with which they communicate issues with their customers. These communities are sometimes part of the web properties managed by companies, however, occasionally they are independently created and grow organically based on shared, common intentions. These forums allow companies to capitalize on the power of common interests between social customers. In creating these forums, companies accept that customer service 2.0 requires reciprocity and collaboration. It also requires trust and transparency, as it fuels engagement by community members. As discussed in preceding chapters, the factor of trust takes on a new life within the era of the social customer.

In examining the community model, different companies will reflect varying degrees of investment in how they structure their total support options. Some companies, like UK telecom provider Giffgaff, have gone for a 100 percent community model that appears to work well. The average speed for an answer in that community is 1.5 minutes. Not only is it fast but customers report being extremely satisfied; after all, they help one another. Verizon, a U.S. telecom provider, maintains all three elements in its support model but capitalizes on the community for ideas through its Idea Exchange. In 2011 they reported that 85 percent of new product features were from ideas received via the forum.

According to the report *State of Social Customer Service 2012,* NM Incite reported that 47 percent of all social media users in the United States had used social care offerings.[38] Seventy percent of those users were satisfied with social care and were inclined to use it again, and 41 percent of those who considered their social care experience unsatisfactory were also prepared to use it again. The social care experience also affects the likelihood of the customer to recommend the brand. Seventy-one percent of those who received great social care were prepared to recommend the brand. Only 17 percent of those who had a somewhat negative experience would recommend the brand. There should be direct correlation between the customer experience strategy and the ultimate support model chosen. Effective execution should drive revenue and reduce costs.

The data, while important, may not always apply universally. However, the principles are consistent with the way customers are normally inclined to operate. The social customer has the potential to have more effect, both positive and negative, in a shorter time frame. With that in mind, the focus on customer service 2.0 must be on more than simply reacting to customer requests. It should embrace the need for proactive elements. As more companies build customer service 2.0 models, they will also realize that the measure of success is not merely in being present on social platforms. It is the degree to which the outcomes of the models implemented meet customer expectations. The appropriate analytics around the customer segment, patterns, and tendencies is important in establishing the appropriate framework.

An interesting development, as part of customer service 2.0, has been the concept of "crowdsourcing," which is becoming increasingly popular and integrated into tools used by customer relationship organizations. Crowdsourcing is defined as "a process that involves outsourcing tasks to a distributed group of people. This process can occur both online and offline. Crowdsourcing is different from ordinary outsourcing since it is a task or problem that is outsourced to an undefined public rather than a specific body."[39] In his book, *Crowdsourcing* (2008), Jeff Howe argues that crowdsourcing has solved the problem of dispersed knowledge and talent. The social media phenomenon has fed the possibility of harnessing capacity to address common issues. This previously did not occur. He highlighted the power of the concept by looking at the ratings and business success achieved by the talent show American Idol. By utilizing the concept, they attract over 80 million votes each season. Many organizations use products like Chatter from Salesforce.com to integrate crowdsourcing into their business processes. It facilitates sharing within a confined community to broaden the source of solutions while promoting participation. Attempts at getting communities involved in these processes are built on the social tendencies and the technologies driving these tendencies. Crowdsourcing fits well within the needs of customer service 2.0.

Knowing the customer

Effective customer service 2.0 models must recognize customers and provide a comprehensive view of who they are. Social customers also want to be known. The lack of physical contact is not an excuse for not knowing a customer in the social era. Good customer data will be critical to enabling satisfactory resolution. This is a key requirement to being successful with customer service 2.0 models. Have you ever entered your telephone number on the request of an IVR, yet the agent does

Donnovan Simon

not know who you? In some cases, they ask for the information again. The design of systems within the model above should include capturing appropriate information to distinguish individuals. It should also account for different customer profiles. The design of tools for the do-it-yourself customer must be robust enough to reflect intelligence about the customer's engagement with the tool. Imagine a web property that has great security and authentication but does not remember the last issue you logged. While the tool may be great, if it delivers an unsatisfactory experience it does more harm than good.

While customer service 2.0 is applicable to all customers, organizations will need to make allowances for the different customer segments they serve. Knowing the customers makes this easier. In the table below, I have applied my perspective on how support options are likely to be adopted by different generations. While there may be variances in different markets, some common elements must be accepted to navigate customer service 2.0. All elements are important in the strategy. It may also be easier and more cost effective to build for the future and appease the current generations. The power of the relationship with customers provides great benefits as organizations implement changes to their support models. The trust factor pays dividends here.

Table 5: Likelihood to utilize customer support options by generation

	Company contact	Self-serve	Community
Baby Boomers	High	Low	Low
Generation X	Moderate	Moderate	Low
Millennials	Low	High	Very High
M2	Very Low	Moderate	Very High

The concept of trust has been part of customer service equations and continues to be important even within the era of the customer service 2.0. However, dimensions change to conform to the characteristics of a virtual, social society. Inherent in the communities and other forums in which customers engage are varying degrees of trust. While customers will take necessary precautions to ensure the safety of their information and privacy, they expect that companies will build trust relationships with customers within the virtual world. A c o n s u m e r purchasing on A m a z o n — a n d there are millions of them—expects the company to deliver and respond to service requests honestly. No conversations or physical interaction occurs, but an inherent

Customer Care from Zappos

Zappos, the booming online retailer, has found a customer support formula that [   ]*eased their customers. They have allowed customer support personnel to be creative, encouraging them to do whatever i* [ ] *required to meet and exceed customer expectations. It is not unlikely that they will have a pizza delivered to a customer who ad* [ ] *that that would make their day. Af* [ ]*l, what is a pizza in the big scheme of things to delight a customer? As an example of Zappos' almost insane customer care, the company has even been known to shop at other stores for customers.*

In 2009, a traveller checked into the Mandalay Bay Hotel and Casino in Las Vegas, Nevada. When the traveller was unpacking she realized that she'd forgotten a pair of her favourite shoes. She had purchased the missing shoes at Zappos, so she headed to its website. When she could [ ]*nd another pair of the same shoes on t* [ ]*te, she called the company's help-desk concierge service. Zappos no longer had the shoes, but its headquarters are located jus* [ ] *outside of Las Vegas, so the Zappos team located the shoes at a nearby mall, went there and purchased the shoes. They then hand-delivered them to the customer at the Mandalay Bay, all at no charge.*

expectation is trusting the other party. Customers also expect to be trusted in these virtual worlds. In fact, the transaction is the beginning of a relationship that has the potential to deliver huge benefits to all involved. I shop online often (you name it, and I have likely purchased it online). I expect the merchant to deliver what was advertised quickly and without bother. I expect the product to be of the quality reflected on the site and should there be an issue, I expect to resolve the issue via an email or some similar method. I am sure they expect me to share my positive experiences with my network or provide reviews or other testimonials within my virtual community. This faceless, voiceless exchange of trust is the norm for customer service 2.0. Some companies, like Zappos, have shown how the correct strategy can work effectively in the era of faceless, voiceless exchanges.[40] It requires companies to develop a clear strategy for customer experience and apply the changes to how key customer interactions and related processes are designed. This could mean changing the traditional scripted approaches to call centres, the employee performance review framework, and the limits of authority policies. It could also be reflected in the removal of restrictions on what customers are permitted to do to support themselves.

Another important element in the customer service 2.0 era is proactivity. It is by no means a new concept as many companies have in the past taken the initiative to reach out to their customers. This has been done through welcome calls or some other basis for contact. With customer service 2.0, proactivity should be done systematically. Through the features in CRM systems, customers can be triaged based on their social profile and appropriate actions taken to delight the customer. Welcome to the era of the social CRM. Proactive customer care

(PCC) has recently become more structured with products and systems being developed to respond quickly to triggers that may impact a customer's experience. The systems are providing information and in some cases solutions to the customer, all geared at making it easier. PCC appeals to a generation driven by speed and urgency. Increasingly, it is a core part of the toolset organizations employ as they attempt to heighten their customers' experiences while managing their operating costs. These tools help companies know their customers more and accede to their preferences. Airlines, public utilities, and retail stores have all found use cases that enable them to activate their PCC systems to both head off potential negative perceptions and generate more bases for loyalty from their customers. Part of this trend is including social media platforms as part of the PCC applications. Customers can communicate through multiple channels including voice, email, SMS, and social media. More sophisticated systems add video as part of their PCC offerings. All these offerings will likely become mainstream and fully integrated into CRM systems to ensure customers receive the treatment they expect and companies derive benefits from their investment. Major benefits to PCC are increased customer engagement, reduced cost, and maintenance of service standards.

While trying to delight customers, companies should accept that the social customer has the opportunity to quickly compare companies and their offerings. They can access comments, reviews, and ratings through social media. To have a successful customer service 2.0 model, it is important to understand how mobile computing makes the landscape different. Have you ever been in a group where you ask a question and the smartphones pop out to research it? Soon you have more information than you had bargained for. You quickly make a decision based on the power of your network and their mobile devices. More customers are way more knowledgeable about the power they can wield because of this access to social networks, and if tested, which sometimes happens, will exercise that option. Support models should effectively cater to this mobility and tendency toward speed and on-demand options.

As technologies evolve, applying deeper customer service 2.0 strategies will be easier through the convergence of tools built to support customer relationships. More systems will focus on social customer needs thereby enabling companies to align their customer experience with developments on social networking platforms. There is a lot more to learn about the social customer, but with so much already happening, it is important for companies to get into the game of operating, and supporting customers, where they are.

CHAPTER 9
Customer Experience Management

There is a buzz around customer experience (CX) as a discipline and I want to highlight the correlations between CX and the themes captured in this book. In *The Way You Make Me Feel: 20 Lessons in Customer Service* (2011), I told stories of how customers, including me, felt, based on the actions of people delivering service in different scenarios. I intended to focus on the emotional elements that are a part of the customer experience equation. Through interacting with organizations and their products, customers (social customers included) have emotional responses. In some cases customers develop emotional ties to brands, and these emotions aggregate and translate into ratings, likes, dislikes, and often, purchasing decisions. In this chapter, I want to raise the awareness about the importance of achieving alignment between the customer's and company's perspectives regarding customer experience. As more investments are made to meet customer expectations, it is critical that the experience delivered by an organization is in sync with how customers rate that experience. The focus on CX management helps organizations achieve that.

Customer experience is defined as the "the sum of all experiences a customer has with a supplier of goods or services, over the duration of their relationship with that supplier."[41] While this definition is true and applicable, deeper aspects to the concept take into account factors that are often considered fluffy and immeasurable. To some, those factors may be determined unimportant. It is important, if not critical, that as strategies for customer experience are developed that a perspective, as expressed by a broader definition, be applied. The definition from customer experience professionals at Beyond Philosophy is most appropriate: "A customer experience is an interaction between an organization and a customer as perceived through a customer's conscious and subconscious mind. It is a blend of an organization's rational performance, the senses stimulated and the emotions evoked and intuitively measured against customer expectations across all moments of contact."[42] This broader perspective ensures that emotional elements are acknowledged. In doing this, it guides business leaders, and others involved in the delivery of products, service, and support to be aware of the basis on which they are likely to be measured by the customer, irrespective of how they measure themselves. This distinction is important in developing correct strategies to meet the customer needs. It also helps to establish an attractive image for potential customers.

In October 2012, I attended the Customer Experience Forum hosted by Forrester Consulting. It was a tremendous event. What impressed me was the level of acceptance demonstrated both by presenters and participants on some fundamental issues. There was general acknowledgement that customers had feelings that mattered and they could and should be measured to gauge the potential impact on business results. There was acceptance that customer experience was not as complex as sometimes perceived, especially since customers, generally, expect some very simple, logical things. It was also good to see that many companies accept that it is not all about technology, customer support applications, or big data. To many companies, it was clear that examining other details and investing in other areas may be the answer to delivering on customer expectations. One example was where a company changed its focus to its customer experience rating (a metric it started to collect) versus its call centre and employee productivity metrics. In doing that, as part of the overall CX strategy, there was greater alignment with key business imperatives. There were also companies that adjusted their approach to having Net Promoter Score (NPS) as the sole measure of the customer's experience. While it was not presented as a wrong approach, light was shed on the need to distill metrics to get a sense of the customer feelings. The most outstanding information from the event, in my mind, was the analysis of the performance of companies that topped the 2012 Customer Experience Index (CXI) collated by Forrester Consulting in the United States. The growth in market value (based on the NASDAQ and NYSE) of the companies at the top of the 2012 CXI was greater than the average performance of the market.[43] Coincidence? Maybe.

None of the items listed above occur within a vacuum and are therefore part of the mix of all the topics discussed in the preceding chapters. Business leaders and professionals on the front line must determine how it all fits into the appropriate strategy and practice for their organization. Additionally, there has to be work to design how it gets executed to derive the outcomes that are expected for the stakeholders in the equation.

No focus on customer experience is complete without accepting that technologies continue to change the business landscape. They also affect customers' experiences and expectations. I could argue that the speed and frequency of these changes, can make investments, which were previously logical, appear obsolete and inappropriate very quickly. We could look at IVR systems as an example of technology that quickly lost relative value with the arrival of advanced knowledge bases, CRM-based customer portals, and other technologies. Have you found an IVR recently that gave you an outstanding experience? Don't they all seem to be focused on the agent and not the customer? Not to mention that when you've made your selections, you are asked for the same information again when you finally get to an agent. Companies that invested in core systems to answer and assist customers found that with time some became sources of frustration and negatively impacted customers' experiences, though there were positive developments in that area of technology. As other technologies have changed and as customers have evolved, what were great self-service ideas delivered through IVRs may no longer match the experience that companies want to deliver.

Customer experience maturity

The extent to which companies understand and meet customer expectations is a function of their maturity with the components required to deliver outstanding experiences. Customer experience maturity is defined by Forrester Consulting as, "the extent to which an organization routinely performs the practices required to design, implement, and manage customer experience in a disciplined way." [44] The principles captured in this and other definitions are key elements of business success strategies. The focus is to have organizations assess their investments across the different phases of the customer life cycle. Additionally, it is to measure the degree to which all parts of the organization are focused and effectively contribute to customer experience outcomes. Similar to maintaining effective personal relationships, customer relationship components have to be systematic and native to an organization. Anything less would make the relationship vulnerable to variations that may occur at an inopportune time. This variability also has the tendency to create doubt. In such cases, the risk of apathy and defection increases.

Different models exist to support organizations focused on customer experience maturity, including a model of assessing customer experience maturity used by Forrester that I find interesting and practical. It assesses six disciplines: Strategy, Customer Understanding, Design, Measurement, Governance, and Culture. These disciplines are assessed based on a four-point scale—Missing, Ad-hoc, Repeatable, and Systematic (MARS).[45] Deeper details in the framework guide users to a summary view of their organization.

Other models, while taking different approaches, all come back to the core intent of assisting companies' focus with greater precision and structure to the requirements of being truly customer focused. The Temkin Group promotes a model with four competencies and a six-stage maturity cycle.[46] This model includes more focus on leadership and the critical role of employees in the ultimate success of CX efforts within an organization. Understandably, the best structured program or model will deliver limited results if the degree of engagement by those leading the required changes are not at the levels neded.

Figure 2: Temkin CX core competencies

Four Customer Experience (CX) Core Competencies

Customer-Centric Organizations
Must Master These Four Competencies

Purposeful Leadership
Do your leaders operate
consistently with a clear,
well articulated set of values?

Compelling Brand Values
Are your brand attributes
driving decisions about
how you treat customers?

CX Competencies

Employee Engagement
Are employees fully
committed to the goals
of your organization?

Customer Connectedness
Is customer feedback
and insight integrated
throughout your organization?

© 2013 Temkin Group

As the focus on gaining benefits from investment in customer experience heats up, numerous indices and reports on the customer perception of major companies are available. These have provided valuable points of reference to companies on how customers feel. While I would argue that there is still some way to go before these indices become mainstream, in the same breath I accept that large sub-sections of influential industries (health care, hospitality, telecommunications, and travel) are taking note. They are applying new components, e.g., new metrics, new executive roles, and new tools to how they operate regarding customer experience. I was in a conversation with a manager of the marketing team at Cisco, who declared that Cisco was in the "customer experience business." Who would have imagined hearing that a few years ago? In fact, some would snicker at that comment today. What role does some huge technology company have in the discipline of customer experience? Is there truly a role for them? The discussion on this could be endless with no correct answer. However, a reasonable conclusion is that there is a place for the convergence of industries and perspectives to address the recognition that customers have increased power through the technologies that have been developed.

Additionally, a reasonable admission is that the focus on the bells and whistles of products has been relegated or more accurately merged with a focus on how customers feel about those bells and whistles. A good example would be Apple. With each product launched by Apple there is usually anticipation and hype. The iPhone 4 was no exception. However, there was material customer dissatisfaction with the performance of the built-in antennas and later with its map application. Yet there was no noticeable mass defection from the Apple brand based on the market share and revenues reported. However, I am sure that the disaffection of the customers was noticed and steps were taken to provide a map application that satisfied customer expectations. The disaffection and by some standards the delayed response or resolution could be attributed to a breakdown in what was previously a systematic business process focused on customer experience.

As the discipline becomes more accepted and mature, more CX models will be developed primarily because the question of how companies do more to deliver services and support to meet customer's expectations remains relevant and necessary. Recently, I watched my daughter, Danielle, who is almost seven years old, try to use a gift card she received on an online children's game site. After numerous unsuccessful attempts to redeem the card, she gave up and suggested moving to another site that had similar games. She had already defected. There was no inclination to try endlessly or go back to the point of purchase or ask for help. Her approach, which granted could be a function of genetics, was to move on to where her need was likely to be satisfied. To me, she had already decided that this was a write-off. The focus on CX models will increase as companies focus more on minimizing the occurrence of these experiences.

The focus on customer experience management has led to more appointments at the executive level with specific responsibility for this area. In recent times, titles that include *customer experience* have become commonplace in all industries. While the skeptic could argue that this is just another professional fad driven by desperation, there are those, including me, who would counter that it is a great business case in adaptation. As competitive forces change and headwinds alter direction and intensity, the need to adapt and adjust has become even more critical. The focus on customer experience is merely one area where this adaptation is more pronounced. Areas such as governance, culture, and financial controls have also seen increased investment in response to the circumstances in the market and within companies. The fact that companies are investing in these areas is a good sign of both corporate responsibility and vision. Corporate leaders who choose to ignore the changing dynamics on the premise that their product is needed and customers are not likely to be more demanding are flirting with decline and in some cases demise.

The journey and ecosystem

While the leadership of customer experience programs is critical, the application must incorporate sound methodologies that include focus on the customer's journey through different engagement processes. Understanding these processes, whether they be web-based or physical, is important to making the required changes to achieved desired results. Also key to the process is understanding the ecosystem or network that supports these processes. The ecosystem includes people, processes, and systems that impact both directly and indirectly the customer's experience with an organization. This includes partners, vendors, and other teams that interact with those responsible for the actual delivery of a good or service. Even for social customers, understanding the impact of the ecosystem is a critical component. Recently, I launched my company's website. The design phase went great and everything was going well until the Internet host had an issue with the mail server. Users of my site, while seeing what I wanted them to see, were not able to send requests from the contact page, which affected their experience with my company. You could say that they should understand that it was not my site that caused the issue, but is that a reasonable expectation? For many organizations whose processes are more complex, the degree to which the customer journey is understood and the ecosystem is defined may determine the achievement of positive results, e.g., support cost reduction, increased net promoter score (NPS), and improved customer experience index (CXI). The ecosystem definition should be followed by appropriate actions to make all involved aware of their role, impact, and value to the customer experience outcomes.

While the investment in understanding and managing customer experience is increasing, many companies still have no comprehensive strategy around customer experience. In many of these companies, the focus is on the customer service team to deliver the "experience." In these cases, the tendency is to position improvement in customer service performance metrics as an improvement in customers' experiences. This is a shallow if not wrong approach.

Recently, I was part of a panel of judges for an awards organization that focuses on excellence in sales and service. As I read through over 100 entries, I was amazed at how many companies are still locked in the era where the speed to answer an inbound call or respond to an email was the hallmark of the quality of the service offered. That was their perspective of customer experience. When I managed support teams, a core part of our philosophy was to clarify that the greatest impact on the experience comes after answering quickly since answering quickly to deliver a sub-par experience was even more damaging. In the end, the focus on seconds, which occurs at the level of the call centre manager, while important, is of little significance to the majority of the customers being engaged. This is not to suggest that operational metrics are irrelevant as they are important to effectively manage the resource requirements and financial viability of such operations. More important is to accept that customer perception is not always influenced by these numbers. There are more significant elements to track and address to consistently deliver the experience customers desire. How customers perceive the ease of getting issues resolved, the sense of value they felt during the interaction, and the degree to which they found the interaction pleasing offer more valuable insight to the company. Extracting value from customer support teams is an important component in effective customer experience management but it is by no means the end-all.

Customer experience management guides the focus of an organization by ensuring that in all areas there is an appreciation of CX goals and how they are achieved. It ensures that the ecosystem of teams, partners, and vendors that contribute to the success of the customer processes are engaged to achieve success. This approach will refocus an organization and allow for more effective analysis and resolution of customer issues. Customer experience management provides a comprehensive model through which to drive growth by delighting customers in a systematic way.

Chapter 10
What Next?

Technology will continue to improve and the social customer will continue to reign. Business leaders, managers, and others involved in guiding customer experience strategies will require practical tools that can be applied to the different scenarios organizations deal with. I would like to summarize the key themes in the book and propose some strategy elements that all organizations and business leaders should consider as they attempt to grapple with social media and its impact on customer experience. The three key takeaways from this work are

- Social media has created a social customer globally
- Customer support strategies must adapt to the new customer personas
- Customer experience will be even more critical to sustained business success

Organizations can adopt varying models to address the needs and expectations of social customers. There is no standard template. To create the customer experience strategy that will deliver the desired outcomes, an organization will need to complete several preparatory steps. Each organization needs to assess, review, analyze, and plan to arrive at the model that best serves its target market. I suggest that companies do the following as part of the process:

a) Develop better demographics around their current customer base—customers want to be known. This should extend beyond the core transaction. This broader profile enables all participants in different stages of the customer experience cycle to contribute more effectively to meeting the customers' expectation. Ultimately knowing and capitalizing on what one knows about the customer will deepen relationships and establish the basis for loyalty. Loyalty becomes revenue.

b) Review existing support models to establish alignment with the demographics gathered—knowing who your existing customers are should provide a platform to review the validity of existing support options. This includes reviewing customer support systems, e.g., CRM tools to determine if they have been optimized or are capable of supporting broader strategies, which could reduce costs.

c) Establish cost bases for support organizations that are ultimately tied to revenue—this could be achieved through the success of loyalty programs, customer experience ratings, or net promoter scores. There should be a direct relationship to both cost avoidance and revenue as part of the budgetary allocation for support organizations.

d) Get social for the right reasons and in the right ways—the establishment of social presence should be integrated into other customer experience strategies and measures established to continuously evaluate the impact of this social presence. Merely launching a Facebook page or Twitter handle will not likely deliver desired results. It would also not increase the customer experience maturity of the organization if these tools are not systematically utilized in the delivery of customer experience.

It is also critical that core operating models precede or accompany the development of customer support strategies. These include clear corporate strategies, defined brand attributes, and clear social media strategies. Influencing all this should be an honest attempt to have the customer at the core of the operating models. Many companies make the claim to customer-centricity, but their core operating models don't reflect that. The inverted triangle following can be used as a starting point for this process.[47] The model proposes a graduated allocation of focus with the customer getting the greatest percentage of the triangle.

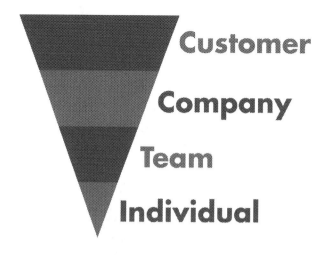

I also want to add some predictions to stimulate the thinking of our business leaders as they determine the next steps in guiding organizations to success in the era of the social customer. There will be more research, reports, and publications related to these issues that can assist organizations in making sound decisions leading to greater success.

Some of the items below may appear simplistic, and that is intentional. Often, obvious, simple items are overlooked in favour of more grandiose ones, which results in re-work and more costs. Some of the issues around customer experience management are table stakes, or at least some would think so, but they are not always evident in organizations.

1. Social networking is here to stay

Should there be skepticism about the likelihood of social media and its derivatives remaining a force, I would counsel strongly against that view. The statistics related to the use of social media are staggering and no signs exist that a new phenomenon will displace it anytime soon. While all businesses in that market segment may not maintain the momentum in accumulating wealth, there is no question more people will find value in joining a virtual community. Clearly, the concept is so innate to the way humans generally operate that uprooting or unseating it is practically impossible. This means that it will gain further significance in the way customers expect to connect.

The principles of trust, engagement, and common interests will serve to drive users of these social platforms to rely more on each other for support. Companies will need to understand and apply appropriate strategies to operate in such an environment. The way mobile carrier Giffgaff has integrated social media in all aspects of their engagement with customers will become normal. Core marketing and support are all done through the communities that have been created. For some, that would be considered very risky or misaligned with other core operating models. That is fine. The all-social model is not for every company, although companies should understand their customer demographics and build models that meet and support them where they are. Clearly, there are rewards when social elements are included than if only traditional models were used.

2. More optimization of smartphones

It is absolutely amazing the convergence that has occurred with mobile technology in recent times. Manufacturers have done much to make these devices friendlier and more functional. They have added more real estate to the screens, in addition to the processing and storage capacity. This has created an opportunity to do more with these devices. Social customers are always finding ways to get more from the social spaces, including interacting with companies they do business with. To get information, these devices will be a standard gateway to their network. In a recent survey of 100 people within my LinkedIn network, approximately 75 percent use a mobile device to access social networking sites. With access to so many friends and colleagues in the palm of a customer's hand, companies must take into account how quickly the impact of an experience could be shared. The multiplier effect of the growth in social customers powered by smartphones and tablets is very powerful. Many opportunities exist in those trends.

3. Millennial behaviour will not change much

There could be a view that the Millennials will get older and no longer create the disruption they currently do. After all, like all the other generations, adjustments will occur as they age. Maybe not! They will likely retain or increase their dependence on social and mobile technologies as they age. They may become more demanding. The benefits that the Millennials derive from technology will also extend their value to businesses as they will more easily maintain pace with changes compared to previous generations. With the improvements and focus on healthy living, Millennials are the generation poised to get the most benefit from new approaches in medicine and other life-extending processes. With those things in mind, it will be normal for that generation to push their value to the limit. The issue of relevance has been core to Millennials and it is unlikely to change. It means that many of the efforts of enterprises will remain focussed on grabbing and maintaining their attention.

4. The next generation (M2) will be even more demanding

If there was a view that Millennials were demanding and stretched the concept of consumer power, that was a practice run for the generation I describe as M2 (Millennials II). Not only will they have been digital natives from birth, they will have been accustomed to a faster, mobile world where products were increasingly cheaper and more powerful. They would also have benefitted from a significant investment in education technology that would make them the *crème de la crème* of education systems in developed economies. This generation would also have had more technology in their home than any previous generation. While some would have had to deal with the impacts of economic instability in major economies, they would also have experienced the greatest level of liberal and pragmatic tendencies in society. They were born as social customers. With all these factors at play, their sense of entitlement will be heightened, as will their expectations of all providers of goods and services.

5. Investment in customer experience solutions will increase

As the global economy continues to sputter toward sustained growth, businesses of all sizes will continue to find ways to improve the basics of their operations, i.e., better cost structures and more sustainable revenue streams. A key component in the equation to achieve these will be dealing with customer experience. Companies that have already started the processes will start deriving benefits, and the success stories will trigger increased focus and investment. There will also be more track record and research on which consulting organizations and other companies can build their offers and rationale for proposed investments. More tools will be developed to support the maturity of the discipline. This is not to suggest that all initiatives will originate external to companies. With social media remaining strong and relevant, sharing experiences will both validate the research and push companies to focus more on their customer experience strategies.

6. More investment in core enterprise applications

There will be a resurgence in investment in core customer relationship applications. The cloud has already become the popular trend and that will continue. Social CRM will find a place. Companies offering products in that space will look to integrate more offerings on already established platforms to ensure greater return on investment (ROI) for enterprises. More focus on customer experience will result in more features and functionality in core applications, which assist companies to reflect customer-centricity. The goal is for these systems to contribute to increased customer retention and satisfaction, which leads to lower costs and increased revenue. What will likely happen is core features will be included that cater to the mobile customer; including the mobile manager. These features, such as embedded survey tools, crowdsourcing apps, knowledge bases, customer experience indices, and others that allow simple analytics will become mainstream. With these features, business leaders will be able to make faster, better decisions. These tools will also do more to reduce the investment in support teams. Some support centres will still remain necessary but more will be done to enable client-side resolution of issues versus intervention by company personnel. These tools will come ready for community deployment to offset the otherwise costly integrations required to achieve that. The CRM business will find a new lease on life.

7. Increased profits through increased consumption

There is already a steady increase in consumption through the Internet. This will continue and will be driven by the fact that access to social customers and customers' access will increase both in the underlying technologies, e.g., 4G and via devices. With more mobile users and more bandwidth, the pipeline of transactions should also expand. As the Millennials earn more and the M2 generation moves into earning mode (however small), the natural inclination to be social and to consume via those platforms will be reflected in consumption numbers. The financial picture for companies that do this well should also improve with many opportunities available to reduce costs by leveraging the power of lower-cost options, e.g., social advertising, social care, and online shopping. I would also argue that the impact of BRIC countries on social customer consumption is yet to be optimized. Once these countries get anywhere close to optimum consumption, the benefits for those actively in the social consumer space should grow.

8. Contact centres will go the way of the mainframe

The reality of the current technologies is that the need for companies to maintain large contact centres will decrease rapidly. This is driven by a range of factors including the proliferation of broadband, the availability of powerful mobile devices, and the propensity for customers to solve issues on their own. While this may be scary to many in the business, as was the view about mainframes three decades ago, the reality of the cost benefits of these support models will catch up with executives sooner than later. Mobile computing allows companies to significantly reduce inbound costs and the operating expense of reactive customer support models. Cost benefits will outweigh the power of the traditional approach. These models will be replaced in major parts by community driven and proactive care models that are a fraction of the current cost and more aligned with the tendencies and preferences of the social customer. In the same breath, the traditional contact centre investment will likely move into more analytics to better enable companies to understand their customers, their actions, and preferences to improve the benefits of positive customer experience.

9. More C-level executives with customer titles

This may seem like an odd thing to say, but it has already started. More leadership teams will agree to the value of being explicit to their customer base about their commitment to improving customer experience. More titles will reflect this. It should not be surprising to see more CEOs adopt some elements of responsibility for this portfolio. Doing this ensures that there is corporate level ownership and governance. Appointments at that level also raise the profile of the ROI and return on effort (ROE) related to customer experience initiatives. The significance of having C-level leadership for customer experience will also show in the realignment and reorientation of businesses, especially those with strong social customer target segments and international footprints. Getting companies to embrace and pivot on the strategic value of customer experience will require that level of leadership.

10. Customer experience differentiation will pay off

We could agree that differentiation in the market place is increasingly difficult if not impossible based on the speed at which change is occurring. The gaps previously evident in product features and quality are being quickly reduced and in some cases eliminated as companies find ways to copy the last new gadget very quickly. With this happening, product differences will be short-lived and so will the premium pricing benefit that the first movers enjoy. As industries move into checkmate, there will be more focus on ensuring a prolonged competitive advantage from customer relationships. This could result in new approaches to loyalty programs, proactive customer care, and pricing. All will be geared at sustaining, for an extended period, the benefit of the differentiation achieved through the delivery of enhanced customer experiences. Studies already show that companies investing in CX strategies perform better than market indices and other companies within their sector. It must be acknowledged that it is still early to draw sweeping conclusions. The trend is healthy and validates some fundamental principles around the power of customer experience on overall company performance.

After all the investments have occurred, the social customer will ultimately derive benefits no other customer persona has. All customer groups will continue to see improvements in the base level of service and the offerings that they receive because of the social customer. The social customer has pushed companies into doing more, including being more public and responsive. The trends may, for some, seem like an ominous picture, for others it will be about the huge opportunities created for companies to derive more business and grow profits. Social customers are active consumers and this trend is likely to increase as they strive to stay with the pace of change in the areas that stimulate them. Be it online shopping or virtual customer management, who knows what the next wave of technology convergence will deliver? The social customer persona will still be driven by the need to be in tandem with what occurs. Additionally, the power of social connections will influence these customers to participate and drive consumption of the things that the community recommends. Today, many sites are driven by referrals, and that will only grow as networks grow. There is, despite the feeling of saturation, way more bandwidth for the Internet and the social networks it supports. With that remains untapped opportunities that first-movers and those focussed on delivering stunning experiences will reap rich rewards from.

As the era of the social customer continues, business leaders must take into account other variables as they move forward. First, the reorientation of business structures. Business leaders must begin to ensure that resources are reinvested in the right areas sooner than later. Organization structures will change based on the efficiency gained from technologies, the incorporation of social tools into supporting customers, and the power of mobile tools. This will lead to retooling of employees, revision of processes, and changes in key performance objectives. Analytics to increase understanding of customer segments will become an area of key focus while contact centre operations reduce. There is a degree of inevitability to the need to invest in social customer support solutions. Often this is not realized or accepted and the delay is ultimately more costly to businesses. It is critical to accept this, restructure and retool, especially in enterprises that are required to drive shareholder value and equity markets.

The other variable that must accompany the reorientation of business structures is the need to accept that the customer has become different in many ways. Many elements of the change have been driven by social media and accompanying technologies. It is by no means a war of winners and losers, as there are little chances of the customer losing. And in cases where it may seem like a loss, it is a temporary situation. Customers have gained ascendency and will remain there because all the foundational pieces (technology, markets, social norms, etc.), support that. It is critical for leaders to support the evolution and drive the appropriate changes within their organizations to ensure alignment with the customer as quickly as possible.

With all of this said, it could be concluded that an era of cyclical confusion awaits us. For those anticipating retirement and more time with their grandchildren, there may be a sigh of relief. For others, including me, there is an air of excitement about the adrenaline-filled, challenging days ahead. For those eager to engage in and contribute to building and executing strategies in such a complex world of technologically savvy, exposed, and social consumers, the fun awaits. The excitement is built on the premise that there is limited room for error and huge opportunity for success. The risk versus reward equation should drive higher levels of engagement, collaboration, and thought. Success is by no means guaranteed, and intent alone will not be enough to engineer success. The key is recognizing the need to make changes and committing to making them and applying the appropriate tools and methods.

There will be those who will see the idea of a social customer and the need to respond as fads that will pass. To that extent, they may argue that the hype is fabricated and will be short lived. While I am tolerant of differing perspectives, from watching my four and seven year old daughters every day, I am deeply convinced that the transformation in customer positioning that has occurred will continue. It will become even more compounded in the years to come. The need for the current generation and future consumers to connect and be catered to will only increase as the foundations become more robust and accommodating of consumer desires. As occurred with the Internet over three generations, where it became pervasive and core, so will social media and its derivatives continue to transform the way the world connects. As this happens, enterprises and businesses of all sizes must adjust, especially with strategies on how they will ensure a fantastic experience for the social customers created by this revolution.

ACKNOWLEDGEMENTS

Completing works like this is not always as simple as it may appear. I used to wonder how hard it could be to write a book. Then I did it and got my answers. In the process, so many people influence, assist, or are asked to invest. It is not always easy to recall and recognize everyone. That said, a few people readily come to top of mind. Friends who I worked with at SMART—Heather, Amy, and Sue—all encouraged and challenged me in different ways. Most importantly, their advice was to go for it.

Kimberley and Donise provided feedback, ideas, and critiqued the manuscript. Taking the time to read the raw ideas and invest time researching and constructing counter proposals to make it a better product was very important. I appreciate their diligence and candid feedback. I am also grateful to Janice, for adding her editing expertise, but more importantly, the willingness to take on the task. I assume all responsibility for the flaws in the final product.

I want to say thanks again to Adam and all the others who filled out my survey and provided perspectives on their social media usage. They allowed me to pry into their practices to provide more substance to my arguments.

The folks at iUniverse were awesome in moving the product through their processes. I appreciate their thorough, professional contributions and patience.

In the end, this book is as much a contribution to the collection of tools for managers and leaders as it is a labour of love and inspiration for my family. My children (Jordin, Danielle, Sydonnae, Michaela, Ashley), whom I love dearly, have been an inspiration to me in so many ways. This, and all my other publications, is dedicated to them and what they mean to me. They represent the highest value that I could contribute to the world. I am sure their generation will surpass the things my generation conceived and delivered. I am convinced they will also do more and achieve more than I have. I am grateful that they allow me the pleasure of influencing their lives, however small. In some ways, I may have deprived them of time and attention while I worked on this book, but I am sure they understand and are fully supportive. I want to express sincere gratitude to Hermalyn, my wife, who like the kids accepted my limited attention without fuss as I focussed on this project. It is nice to know her support was always there.

Professionals all over the world have spent time searching for answers that helped me as I put this book together. I want to acknowledge and recognize those contributions. May you continue to add value to an exciting, challenge-filled world.

APPENDICES

APPENDIX 1
My Survey Results

I sent this survey to 100 people and there were 79 respondents.. All members of the sample were part of my LinkedIn network and were selected randomly. The survey was open for two weeks in January 2013. None of the questions in the survey were mandatory. The minimum number of responses to any question was 75.

Question 1: Which social networking website do you use most often?

Facebook	63.3%
Twitter	19%
LinkedIn	49.4%
YouTube	25.3%

Note: Respondents also listed WeChat, Tumblr, Pinterest, and Instagram as sites they used most often.

Donnovan Simon

Question 2: Do you create or consume content for these sites?

Consume only	59.5%
Both	40.5%

Question 3: Do you respond to advertising on social networking sites?

Yes	16.5%
No	83.5%

Question 4: How often do you visit social networking websites?

Extremely often	24.1%
Very often	31.6%
Moderately often	29.1%
Slightly often	8.9%
Not at all often	6.3%

Question 5: What is your primary purpose for using social networking sites?

Connecting with friends	57.3%
News and information	10.7%
Sharing ideas	20.0%
Entertainment	12.0%

Note: Respondents also listed maintaining business contacts and networking as other primary purposes.

Question 6: Do you use your mobile device to access social networking sites?

Yes	81.0%
No	19.0%

Question 7: Age category

18-20	1.3%
21-29	6.6%
30-39	39.5%
40-49	40.8%
50-59	10.5%
60+	1.3%

Question 8: Gender

Female	53.8%
Male	46.2%

APPENDIX 2
Description of
Top 10 Social Networking Sites

1. **Facebook** (NASDAQ: FB) is a social networking service and website launched in February 2004, operated and owned by Facebook Inc. The social networking company held its initial public offering (IPO) May 18, 2012. The IPO was one of the biggest in technology and the biggest in Internet history with a peak market capitalization of over US$104 billion. Media pundits called it a "cultural touchstone." As of September 2012, Facebook had more than one billion active users._Participants must register before using the site, after which they may create a personal profile, add other users as friends, and exchange messages, including automatic notifications when they update their profile. Additionally, users may join common-interest user groups, organized by workplace, school, college, or other characteristics, and categorize their friends into lists such as "People From Work" or "Close Friends." The name of the service stems from the colloquial name for the book given to students at the start of the academic year by some university

administrations in the United States to help students get to know each other. Facebook allows any users who declare themselves to be at least 13 years old to be register on the site.

2. **Qzone** (Chinese: QQ空间) is a social networking website created by Tencent in 2005. It permits users to write blogs, keep diaries, send photos, and listen to music. Users can set their Qzone background and select accessories based on their preferences so that every Qzone is customized to the individual member's taste.

3. **Twitter** is an online social networking service and microblogging service that enables its users to send and read text-based posts of up to 140 characters, known as "tweets." It was created in March 2006 by Jack Dorsey and launched that July. The service rapidly gained worldwide popularity, with over 140 million active users as of 2012, generating over 340 million tweets daily and handling over 1.6 billion search queries per daily. It has been described as "the SMS of the Internet." Unregistered users can read the tweets, while registered users can post tweets through the website interface, SMS, or a range of apps for mobile devices.

4. **Google+** integrates social services such as Google Profiles and introduces new services identified as Circles, Hangouts, and Sparks. Google+ is available as a website and on mobile devices. Sources such as *The New York Times* have declared it Google's biggest attempt to rival the social network Facebook, which has over 800 million users. Google+ is considered the company's fourth foray into social

networking, following Google Buzz (launched 2010, retired in 2011), Google Friend Connect (launched 2008, retired by March 2012) and Orkut (launched in 2004, now operated entirely by subsidiary Google Brazil). The service was launched as an invitation-only "field test." Early invitations were soon suspended due to an "insane demand" for new accounts. On September 20, 2011, Google+ was opened to everyone 18 years of age or older without the need for an invitation. It was opened for a younger age group (13+ years old in the United States and most countries, 14+ in South Korea and Spain, 16+ in Netherlands) on January 26, 2012.

5. **Habbo** (previously known as Habbo Hotel) is a social networking site aimed at teenagers. The website is owned and operated by Sulake Corporation. The service began in 2000 and has expanded to include 11 online communities (or "hotels"), with users in over 150 countries. However, in April 2012 it was announced that a new hotel would open aimed at users from Turkey. As of August 2011, over 230 million avatars have been registered. There are an average 10 million unique visitors monthly.

6. **LinkedIn** (NYSE: LNKD) is a business-related social networking site. Founded in December 2002 and launched in May 2003, it is mainly used for professional networking. As of February 9, 2012, LinkedIn reported more than 150 million registered users in more than 200 countries and territories. The site is available in English, French, German, Italian, Portuguese, Spanish, Swedish, Romanian, Russian, Turkish, Japanese, Czech, and Polish. Quantcast reports LinkedIn has 21.4 million monthly unique U.S. visitors

and 47.6 million globally. In June 2011, LinkedIn had 33.9 million unique visitors, up 63 percent from a year earlier and surpassing MySpace. LinkedIn filed for an initial public offering in January 2011 and traded its first shares on May 19, 2011, under the NYSE symbol "LNKD."

7. The **Renren Network** (Chinese: 人人网; literally "Everyone's Website"), formerly known as **Xiaonei Network** (Chinese: 校内网; literally "on-campus network") is a Chinese social networking service that is similar to Facebook. It has been called the Facebook of China. It is popular among college students in China. In February 2011, Renren made a pre-IPO announcement that it had 160 million registered users. Then in April 2011, it had to modify that statement to "a total of 31 million active monthly users." The site has had to comply with prohibitions on content enforced by the Chinese government.

8. **Badoo** is a social discovery website founded in 2006. It is managed out of its Soho, London headquarters, but owned by a company in Cyprus and ultimately by Russian entrepreneur Andrey Andreev. In September 2011, *The Economist* wrote an article explaining how Badoo has a shot at becoming "one of Europe's leading Internet firms" and that Badoo seems to have discovered a large new market. The site operates in 180 countries and is most active in Latin America, Spain, Italy, and France. Badoo ranks as the 52nd most popular site in France and the 117th globally, according to Alexa Internet. In July 2011, Badoo.com ranked as the 59th most visited website in the world with 46 million unique visitors per month, ahead of CNN.com

in 60th position. Badoo grows by 150,000 new registrations per day

9. **Bebo** is a social networking website launched in July 2005. It is currently owned and operated by Criterion Capital Partners after taking over from AOL in June 2010. The website's name is an acronym for Blog Early, Blog Often Users receive a personal profile page where they can post blogs, photographs, music, videos, and questionnaires to which other users may answer. Additionally, users may add others as friends and send them messages, and update their personal profiles to notify friends about themselves. Bebo is very similar to other social networking sites, mainly Facebook.

10. **VK** (Originally **VKontakte**, Russian: ВКонтакте) is a Russian social network service popular in Russia, Ukraine, Kazakhstan, Moldova, and Belarus. VK offers a striking similarity in design and functionality to Facebook and as such has been described as a "Facebook clone." Like Facebook, VK allows users to message contacts publicly or privately, create groups, public pages and events, make notes, share and tag images and video, and play browser-based games. One distinction of VK is its integration with torrent file-sharing technology that allows users to share large files. As of March 2012, VK had 118.8 million accounts but has acknowledged that it has a major spam problem and no longer advertises user numbers on its homepage. VKontakte is ranked 46 in Alexa's global Top 500 sites and is the fourth most visited website in Russia. In January 2012, vkontakte.ru was visited by 25.4 million people from Russia (58.7 percent aged 12-54) and vk.com by 21.5 million (49.6 percent aged 12-54).

Works Cited

Books

Howe, Jeff, *Crowdsourcing: Why the Power of the Crowd is Driving the Future of Business,* Three Rivers Press, New York, 2008

Kelly, Kevin, *New Rules for the New Economy,* Viking Penguin, New York, 1998

Schawbel, Dan, *ME2.0:4 Steps to Building Your Future,* Kaplan, New York, 2010

Simon, Donnovan, *The Way You Make Me Feel,* iUniverse, Bloomington, 2011

Papers/Articles/Reports

Bruce Temkin, *The Four Customer Experience Core Competencies: Building Your Path to Customer Loyalty,* The Temkin Group, January 2013

China Internet Watch, *China Social Media Whitepaper,* October 2012, chinainternetwatch.com/whitepaper/china-social-media/

David A. Kaplan, *Howard Schultz brews Strong Coffee at Starbucks, Fortune* Magazine, December 2011, Vol. 164, No. 9

Karen Myers and Kamyab Sadaghiani, *Millennials in the Workplace: A Communication Perspective on Millennials'*

Organizational Relationships and Performance, Journal of Business and Psychology, Volume 25, Issue 2, 2010

Megan Burns, *Customer Experience Maturity Defined,* Forrester Consulting, September 2012

Michael Brito, *The Rise of the Social Customer And Their Impact on Business,* presented at Social Media Bootcamp hosted by Mediabistro, February 16, 2012

Nate Elliott and Gina Sverdlov, *Global Social Media Adoption In 2011: A Social Computing Report,* Forrester Consulting, 2012

NM Incite, *The Social Media Report 2012,* accessed March 2013, nielsen.com/us/en/reports/2012/state-of-the-media-the-social-media-report-2012.html

NM Incite, *The State of Social Customer Service 2012,* accessed March 2013, slideshare.net/NMIncite/state-of-social-customer-service-2012

Rachel Tran, *Why Social Customer Service Matters,* July 2012, accessed March 2013, socialbusinessnews.com/why-social-customer-service-matters/

Richard Darell, *The Evolution of Smartphones,* 2012, accessed March 2013, bitrebels.com/technology/the-evolution-of-smartphones-infographic/

The Swing Group, *Effective Customer Referral through Social Media Marketing,* March 2012, accessed March 2013, slideshare.net/SwingGroup/effective-customer-referral-through-social-media-marketing

NOTES

Web 2.0 is the move toward a more social, collaborative, interactive, and responsive web. It is a change in the philosophy of web companies and web developers, but more than that, Web 2.0 is a change in the philosophy of society as a whole.

Chapter 1

2 Michael Brito is the author of *Smart Business, Social Business,* Pearson Education, 2012, and a prolific contributor to issues related to social customer service and social media. The presentation referenced was for the Social Media Bootcamp hosted by MediaBistro in 2012.

3 In an article, *Why Social Customer Service Matters* (July 2012) on socialbusinessnews.com, Rachel Tran presents views on why companies should use social media as part of their customer support offering.

4 This was part of an infographic on socialbusinessnews.com, which attributed the post to Rachel Tran, Enterprise Business Representative at Conversocial, a Social CRM technology solution.

5 China Internet Watch (CIW) provides reports and analysis on Internet activity in China. While data on Internet usage in China is

sometimes dubious, the trends from CIW are generally consistent with that from other sources such as NM Incite.

Chapter 2

6   Information taken from Google's annual reports listed on their investor page.

7   eMarketer is a company in the United States that evaluates data on media trends. The forecasts provided are contained in a series of reports published by the company periodically. I make no claims to the accuracy or validity of the forecasts provided by eMarketer, even though there is a reasonable basis on which these reports are developed.

8   I conducted a survey with 100 members of my LinkedIn network. The survey, which allowed anonymous responses, had a 70+% response rate. While by no means representative of all users of social networks, the findings were indicative of other commonly validated perspectives about the use of social networking sites. Details on the survey are in Appendix 1.

9   Through the survey I conducted, approximately 60% of respondents cited themselves as only consumers on social media. Forrester Consulting published a report (Global Social Technographics Update 2011) where they reported that there are regional differences in how social media is used from a creation vs. consumption perspective. In the United States and Europe approximately 25% are creators versus in India (80%) or China (76%).

Chapter 3

10   Facebook went public in 2012, listed on NASDAQ. The market capitalization at IPO was US$37 billion, making it the largest technology IPO ever.

¹¹ The data for this table comes from multiple sources including company websites, e.g., Facebook, Sulake, press releases, and other items from news media. The data on Chinese sites comes from the reports from China Internet Watch (CIW) and iresearchchina.com. While I accept that all the user data may not be absolutely perfect, the ranking of these sites is reasonably accurate.

¹² This data focuses on registered users only. The degree to which these users are active has been discussed in many forums, and it is accepted that the data on registered users when compared to active users could change the ranking of these sites, in some cases significantly. Interestingly, many new, growing sites, e.g., Pinterest, may have a significantly higher rate of active to registered users than older sites such as Habbo or QZone.

¹³ The data on smartphone use comes from mobiThinking. com. mobiThinking has sourced their data from the country's telecommunications regulator, association, etc., or directly from the operators. If unavailable, or if more up-to-date material is available, data from analysts has been used. Most of the 3G subscriber stats were provided by Informa WCIS.

¹⁴ The data from IDC shows tremendous growth in the smartphone market with a forecast for sustained growth through to 2015.

¹⁵ eMarketer published a report, *Why Tablet Users are a Retailers Dream*, in 2012 providing data from comscore.com, digitalmarketinginsights.com, prospermobile.com, and emarketer. com.

¹⁶ *Publicness* is the degree to which companies are challenged to maintain public profiles, including providing information that prior to the universal impact of social media would have been maintained internally by companies. Being in the public space

means companies are also "searchable." It is considered normal to go to Google to get information on all targets.

17   This count was as of April 2013.

Chapter 4

18   These are common terms used in SMS or instant messaging conversations that personify actions or phrases but save on characters used while clearly communicating intent. LOL—laugh out loud, OMG—oh my God, and BTW—by the way.

19   Twitter has established a limit for tweets of 140 characters only, requiring users to keep to short expressions.

20   Data on Twitter activity comes from Twitter's blog on their corporate website: www.twitter.com.

21   NM Incite is a joint venture between Nielsen and McKinsey and provides research on numerous areas of social media and related sectors. The report *State of the Media: The Social Media Report 2012* was based on a survey of 1998 U.S.-based social media users between February and July 2012.

22   Cone Communications conducted research on the behaviour of social media users regarding customer support expectations.

23   The Boston Consulting Group (BCG) publishes reports on ecommerce and related activities globally. Their report of 2011 analyzed the ecommerce trends in the United Kingdom.

Chapter 5

24   The Silent Generation refers to people born between 1920 and the 1940s who were affected by the Great Depression. Baby Boomers refers to people born between the mid-1940s and the mid-1960s based on post-World War II population growth. Generation X refers to people born in the mid 1960s through to the early 1980s.

Generation X (also called Millennials and Echo Boomers) were people born in the late 1980s to 2000.

25 During the Clinton administration, the U.S. economy grew by an average of 4% annually, grew for 116 consecutive months, saw median family income increase, and recorded the lowest levels of unemployment for 30 years.

26 Karen Myers and Kamyab Sadaghiani wrote a paper entitled *Millennials in the Workplace: A Communication Perspective on Millennials' Organizational Relationships and Performance* where they focussed on numerous studies and perspectives on how the generation fit within current workplace culture and they challenge they and other generations faced in the relationships that existed.

27 A webbot is a web-based tool that allows a customer to interact with an automated agent (robot) to address support requirements. Through its interactive properties, the webbot is able to respond to keywords and input from the customer to simulate a real-life experience as part of the process of resolving the customer issue.

28 In Dan Schawbel's book, *ME 2.0:4 Steps to Building Your Future,* Kaplan Publishing, New York, 2010, Schawbel outlines the provisions made by these and other companies to respond to the unique features that Gen Y professionals take to the workforce.

Chapter 6

29 Forrester Consulting developed a report that tracked the adoption of social media in 2006. The report, authored by Nate Elliott and Gina Sverdlov, provides a profile on social media trends across different demographic groups across different regions.

30 This information is based on *World Development Indicators* provided by the World Bank.

31 The report *Why Tablet Users are a Retailers Dream* by eMarketer was published in 2012 (*http://tabtimes.com/news/ittech-stats-*

research/2012/04/02/why-tablet-users-are-retailers-dream-infographic) and focussed on the impact of shoppers in different demographics using different devices to complete online transactions.

32   Starbucks has recorded net income increases of approximately US$1B annually for the last four fiscal years with an operating margin of approximately 15%. Net income at end of the 2012 fiscal year was US$13.3B. There has also been steady growth in the number of stores in operation with a target of approximately 20,000 by fiscal year 2016. At the end of the 2012 fiscal year, 18,066 stores were in operation.

33   Howard Shultz was recognized as *Fortune* magazine's Business Person of the Year 2011. A full article, *Howard Schultz Brews Strong Coffee at Starbucks* by David A. Kaplan features excerpts from an interview with him and highlighted the December 2011 (Vol 164, No. 9) edition.

Chapter 7

34   Sephora is a French consumer goods company focussed on cosmetic and beauty products founded in 1970. They recorded revenue of EU€1.2 billion in 2012.

35   The Swing Group is a European consulting firm that produced a report on *Effective Customer Referral through Social Media Marketing* (March 2012).

36   Metcalfe's Law, developed by engineer Robert Metcalfe, proposed that the community value of a network grows exponentially as the square of the number of its users increases. In the world of social media, the impact of the proliferation of users creates significant value for social media platforms. Metcalfe was credited with the invention of Ethernet.

Chapter 8

[37] Reported by Business Time.com, NM Incite's report on Social Customer 2012 showed that over 50% of online users are willing to receive support online.

[38] NM Incite is a joint venture between Nielsen and McKinsey. Their report on social media and social customer care (*The State of Social Customer Service 2012*) was based on a survey of 2000 U.S. social media users. The survey was conducted in July 2012.

[39] Based on a definition from Wikipedia. There are many other interpretations for the concept.

[40] The story in the box was referenced by Armando Roggio in his article *The Zappos Effect: 5 Great Customer Service Ideas for Small Business* (March 2011). The article was on Practical Ecommerce.com, with numerous other stories about Zappos' approach to customer support.

Chapter 9

[41] This definition is from the Customer Experience Maturity model developed by Forrester Consulting.

[42] Beyond Philosophy is a consulting firm in the United States that focuses on customer experience. Their definition is part of the differentiation they offer clients in improving customer experience.

[43] The report shared by Forrester showed that the average financial performance (growth in market value of stocks) for companies in the top quadrant of Forrester's annual Customer Experience Index (2012) outperformed the markets they were listed on. The report is based on surveys of approximately 7,600 companies in the United States across 13 industries.

[44] From *Customer Experience Maturity Defined* (September 2012) published by Forrester Consulting.

45   In the research paper *Customer Experience Maturity Defined* (September 2011), Megan Burns outlines the different disciplines in the CXM model and how each is assessed.

46   The Temkin Group in its report *The Four Customer Experience Core Competencies: Building Your Path to Customer Loyalty* (January 2013), provides insight into the role of Purposeful Leadership, Employee Engagement, Compelling Brand Values, and Customer Connectedness for the achievement of customer experience maturity within an organization. Like Forrester Consulting, the Temkin Group focuses on CXM and has completed numerous reports and studies on the practice mainly in North America.

Chapter 10

47   The concept behind this triangle is credited to my previous manager Sandra Coates as part of her articulation of how our previous organization needed to approach how teams focussed on core issues and initiatives to be truly customer focused.